YEAR ONE

Lighting the path on your
first year in teaching

Michael Chiles &
David Goodwin

First published 2022

by John Catt Educational Ltd,
15 Riduna Park, Station Road,
Melton, Woodbridge IP12 1QT

Tel: +44 (0) 1394 389850
Email: enquiries@johncatt.com
Website: www.johncatt.com

ISBN: 978 1 915261 19 9

Set and designed by John Catt Educational Limited

MICHAEL CHILES

Michael's career began as a geography teacher in a secondary school in the West Midlands where he became head of department and then a senior leader with responsibility for teaching and learning. After relocating to the north-west, he took a short period out of the classroom to develop and deliver teacher training both nationally and internationally. Michael is now a senior leader in a secondary school in the north-west and a council member for the Chartered College of Teaching. He has also written *The CRAFT of Assessment* and *The Feedback Pendulum*. Married to Sarah, with whom he shares two teenage children, Abigail and Harry, and Daisy, the border collie, Michael enjoys walks through the British countryside and playing the guitar.

DAVID GOODWIN

David Goodwin is an assistant principal, a geography teacher, and a writer and illustrator of education ideas. He is also a specialist leader of education (SLE) and evidence lead in education (ELE). His debut book, co-authored with Oliver Caviglioli, was *Organise Ideas: Thinking by Hand, Extending the Mind*. He also wrote and illustrated *Annie Murphy Paul's the Extended Mind in Action* alongside Emma Turner and Oliver Caviglioli. David is married to Marie, and they have a daughter called Maddison. They enjoy spending time in Robin Hood's Bay, where they got married. You can find David on Twitter @MrGoodwin23.

GUEST AUTHORS

Introducing our guest authors, without whom, this book would not have been possible. Collaborating with such dedicated educators has been an honour.

Amy Lyon

History teacher

Clarry Simpson

ECT induction lead and geography teacher

David Morgan

PE curriculum leader

Dawn Cox

Head of RE

Drew Wicken

Director of design and technology

Justin Wakefield

Vice principal

Karl McGrath

Year 5 teacher and task design and curriculum implementation lead

Kate Jones

Senior associate for teaching and learning with evidence-based education

Katherine Walsh

Trust lead for inclusion

Keavy Lowden

English teacher

Nicky Blackford

Assistant headteacher and dance specialist

Dr Poppy Gibson

Senior lecturer and course lead in primary education

Rebecca Chadwick

Lead practitioner of history

Sam Lawrence

Assistant principal, director of pastoral systems

Sarah Jones

Subject leader for business, economics and finance

Emma Turner

Research and CPD lead

Jade Hickin

Trust-wide lead practitioner in English

Jo Baker

Assistant principal and art teacher

Jo Castelino

Second in science and teaching and learning lead

John Hough

Assistant head of secondary education

Kirsten Johnson

Head of music and drama

Laura Pellegrino

Team leader for KS3 geography

Professor Michael Green

Associate executive director of strategic development

Molly McDonough

Head of geography

Nicholas Sermon

Primary phase class teacher and music lead

Shannon McCarthy

Art teacher

Simon Cox

Director of Blackpool Research School

CONTENTS

04

CURRICULUM & ASSESSMENT

The curriculum is the heartbeat of all schools. Learn about types of knowledge, assessment, feedback and why reading is every teacher's responsibility. Also, pick up some tips on designing resources that consider cognitive load theory.

05

PASTORAL

The pastoral chapter covers teachers' wider responsibility, from safeguarding to PSHE and enrichment. You will read strategies for managing parental phone calls and making the most of parents' evenings.

06

PROFESSIONAL DEVELOPMENT

Read how to prepare for your first interview, how to write a personal statement and how to engage in educational research. Also, discover how to manage your own health and wellbeing.

REFERENCES & APPENDICES

The appendix contains the Early Career Framework and Teachers' Standards for your reference while reading this book.

THE ECF MAPPED

	CHAPTER 01 CLASSROOM SYSTEMS	CHAPTER 02 SUBJECT KNOWLEDGE	CHAPTER 03 PEDAGOGICAL PRINCIPLES
STANDARD 01: HIGH EXPECTATIONS	SPREAD 01 | SPREAD 02 | SPREAD 03 | SPREAD 04 | SPREAD 05 | SPREAD 06 | SPREAD 07	SPREAD 08	SPREAD 29 | SPREAD 30
STANDARD 02: HOW PUPILS LEARN	SPREAD 01 | SPREAD 07	SPREAD 08 | SPREADS 09-22	SPREAD 23 | SPREAD 24 | SPREAD 25 | SPREAD 26 | SPREAD 27 | SPREAD 28 | SPREAD 31
STANDARD 03: SUBJECT AND CURRICULUM		SPREAD 08 | SPREADS 09-22	SPREAD 25 | SPREAD 27 | SPREAD 28 | SPREAD 29 | SPREAD 30
STANDARD 04: CLASSROOM PRACTICE	SPREAD 01 | SPREAD 07		SPREAD 23 | SPREAD 24 | SPREAD 25 | SPREAD 26 | SPREAD 27 | SPREAD 28 | SPREAD 31
STANDARD 05: ADAPTIVE TEACHING	SPREAD 02 | SPREAD 03 | SPREAD 05 | SPREAD 06		SPREAD 24 | SPREAD 25 | SPREAD 26 | SPREAD 27 | SPREAD 29 | SPREAD 30
STANDARD 06: ASSESSMENT	SPREAD 03 | SPREAD 06		
STANDARD 07: MANAGING BEHAVIOUR	SPREAD 01 | SPREAD 02 | SPREAD 03 | SPREAD 04 | SPREAD 05 | SPREAD 06 | SPREAD 07		
STANDARD 08: PROFESSIONAL BEHAVIOURS			SPREAD 29 | SPREAD 30

To help you get the most out of *Year One*, we have carefully mapped each double-page spread against the Early Career Framework. Use this to shape your desired reading route or to dip in and out of the book as you need.

CHAPTER 04 CURRICULUM & ASSESSMENT	CHAPTER 05 PASTORAL	CHAPTER 06 PROFESSIONAL DEVELOPMENT
SPREAD 36 | SPREAD 41 | SPREAD 42 | SPREAD 43 | SPREAD 44	SPREAD 46 | SPREAD 47 | SPREAD 48 | SPREAD 50 | SPREAD 51	SPREAD 61 | SPREAD 64
SPREAD 34 | SPREAD 35 | SPREAD 37 | SPREAD 38 | SPREAD 39 | SPREAD 41 | SPREAD 45		SPREAD 54 | SPREAD 59 | SPREAD 62 | SPREAD 63
SPREAD 34 | SPREAD 37 | SPREAD 38 | SPREAD 42 | SPREAD 43		SPREAD 54 | SPREAD 56 | SPREAD 57 | SPREAD 59 | SPREAD 62 | SPREAD 63
SPREAD 35 | SPREAD 37 | SPREAD 38 | SPREAD 39		SPREAD 54 | SPREAD 59 | SPREAD 62 | SPREAD 63
SPREAD 37 | SPREAD 38 | SPREAD 39 | SPREAD 44		SPREAD 54 | SPREAD 59
SPREAD 35 | SPREAD 37 | SPREAD 38 | SPREAD 39		
	SPREAD 46 | SPREAD 47 | SPREAD 48 | SPREAD 49 | SPREAD 50 | SPREAD 51	
		SPREAD 52 | SPREAD 53 | SPREAD 55 | SPREAD 56 | SPREAD 57 | SPREAD 58 | SPREAD 60

THE EARLY CAREER FRAMEWORK CAN BE FOUND IN APPENDIX A OF THIS BOOK

SONIA THOMPSON
Headteacher and director

As I read this book, I actually wished I was an ECT all over again, as knowing its contents would certainly have made my early teaching life that much easier. The writers show an acute grasp of what the new, busy teacher needs to know. In doing so, they present their audience with an exceptionally well-researched and accessible book, for all phases. Each chapter dissects the crucial components of teaching pedagogy and practice. It is done in such a way that the reader not only learns but also deepens their knowledge. Everything on every page is intentional and accessible, and each quote and referenced writer serves to further affect the reader experience. If this is one of the only books the busy ECT reads in Year One, it will be more than enough and then some.

PEPS MCCREA
Dean at Ambition Institute

Year One is the Wagamama of teaching books. It looks stunning, is packed with great ingredients, and leaves you both satisfied yet hungry for more!

TOM BENNETT
Behaviour advisor to the DfE, founder of researchED

This is a lovely book. At last, after so many years of beginning teachers burdened like donkeys by apocryphal how-to guides written, apparently, by Martians, we have a new generation of training resources bursting with practical advice, evidence-informed strategies, and what we need to know rather than what some Kafkaesque mandarin of education thinks you should be thinking about. This book would sit well on any CPD shelf.

JADE PEARCE
Assistant headteacher for teaching and learning and CPD

This is the book that all early career teachers need to read. It covers all of the aspects of a teacher's role. All are explained clearly and succinctly with both references to research and practical experience and applications for the classroom. In short, it will allow all readers to make an excellent start to their teaching career and is the book I wish I had access to at the start of my own journey.

EMMA TURNER
Research and CPD lead

There are some books that are sure to become instant classics. *Year One* falls into that category: easy to read, accessible, covering both the basics and the more complex and challenging. It provides a compendium of professional advice and combines wisdom from across the sector, all crafted carefully by David and Michael to produce a highly useful guide, which is also beautiful to navigate. This book is mentor, cheerleader, professional friend, coach and tutor; a superb literary warm welcome to the profession for early career teachers.

SUFIAN SADIQ
Director of Teaching School

If I could turn back time and start my career again, the one thing I know for sure is that I would always have this book within reach. Having read this cover to cover, I know this will be the book I recommend to our ITT students and our ECTs. It is simple, easy to follow and, for a busy teacher, it captures all the essential information from a dozen books all in one. It is a great resource for mentors to use and reference when working with teachers.

MARY MYATT
Education writer and speaker

An incredibly helpful resource for early career teachers; tight, to the point, and a terrific balance of important research headlines and practical strategies to keep sane in the early years of teaching.

WES DAVIES
CEO of The Two Counties Trust

Wow, just what every new teacher needs! It is more than a guide; the authors have created a companion that can be picked up as and when needed, dipped in and out of in whatever time you have. *Year One* provides a highly practical and research-informed companion for those new to the profession. The range of topics covered includes pastoral elements, subject-specific guidance, pedagogical choices, and lots of practical points. This makes the book highly unique. Despite being a concise read it is incredibly informative and the material is not diluted.

FOREWORD

Haili Hughes is head of education at IRIS Connect, a senior lecturer and teacher development mentor lead at the University of Sunderland, journalist, speaker and author.

HAILI HUGHES

Teaching is an incredibly complex activity – simultaneously both an art and a science. It is not a technician's checklist but there are certain essential elements of effective teaching that every new teacher should know about and can be mastered through practice.

These strategies, underpinned by robust research, can act as best bets to help early career teachers (ECTs) become more effective teachers and give our students the education they deserve. To do this, as well as a deep subject content knowledge, new teachers need a thorough understanding of pedagogical knowledge to be able to develop their professional knowledge, skills and judgement. Yet on top of the demands of a heavy teaching timetable, getting to grips with marking and the sheer cognitive load that the school environment brings with it, reading and understanding the practical implications of research in a meaningful way can seem like an impossible task.

Luckily, this book is a brilliant companion to what can sometimes be a difficult year. It seamlessly integrates theory with practice, in a digestible and attractive way, which can be dipped into time and time again throughout the year. With a clear focus on standards and tangible take away strategies from education experts who've served their time at the coalface, it frees ECTs up to work on their teaching and hone their craft, using the evidence in the book to underpin their professional judgement and guide their reflections.

I have often said that there is no manual for teaching but in this case, I am happy to be proved wrong. What Michael Chiles and David Goodwin have achieved in the writing of this book will leave a lasting legacy on the profession; we need to support our most vulnerable staff, our ECTs, as much as possible, and this is a great start.

FOREWORD

Abby is executive director of the Greenwood Academies
Trust Institute of Teaching, speaker and author.

We are so lucky to have a plethora of research, education
books and advice at our fingertips. However, as a trust CPD
lead, early career teachers often feedback that this can, at
times, feel overwhelming, making it difficult to know where
to start and where to head next. *Year One: Lighting the path
on your first year in teaching* delivers on its promising title,
offering a neat synthesis of seminal advice, further reading
and important pedagogy that will form a solid foundation
for all early career teachers' CPD.

ABBY BAYFORD

Every teacher can relate to the feeling of having so much
to learn. What struck me when reading this book is that
it is ultra-concise and accessible, ensuring the glass never
feels too full. The chapters have been carefully ordered
to sequence knowledge in a way that builds. Moreover,
sections are structured to impart powerful knowledge
and synthesise underpinning research and pedagogy. In a
nutshell, the book is a treasure trove of seminal thinkers,
pedagogy principles and implementation suggestions
structured to make CPD manageable for teachers joining
the profession.

One of the common persistent challenges I face as a
strategic lead for early career teacher development is that
CPD often meets with teachers outside the classroom,
making the application of ideas hard. This book ensures
implementation is not left to chance through scripted
scenarios that bring the pedagogy and research to life.

Year One: Lighting the path on your first year in teaching
is not just packed with knowledge, it is also a humbling
read. The exploration of common pitfalls articulated as
'hidden hurdles' remind us that teaching really is a human
endeavour and we will never fully crack it! I am sure it
will resonate with many and become root and branch of
early career teacher development. In fact, I fully intend to
use this book as an infrastructure for every teacher's CPD
curriculum in our trust.

CLASSROOM SYSTEMS

01

HIGH EXPECTATIONS

To have high expectations of all students is to show you care. It means you have to be consistent in expecting the same behaviours of all.

02
SPREAD | P.18

STRONG START

A strong start to a lesson sets the foundations for purposeful learning and a calm environment.

03
SPREAD | P.20

ESTABLISHING ROUTINES

Whether it is the start, ending or transition between activities, routines create safe, caring and productive learning environments.

04
SPREAD | P.22

BUILDING RELATIONSHIPS

The teacher–student relationship is one of the most powerful levers for establishing a productive learning environment.

01

HIGH EXPECTATIONS

To have high expectations of all students is to show you care. It means you have to be consistent in expecting the same behaviours of all.

The cognitive dissonance of high expectations

The phrase 'high expectations' is ubiquitous in education. You will see it in educational policies, schools' ethos and vision statements, and you'd be hard-pressed to find a teacher who doesn't claim to have high expectations of their students. And yet, according to behaviour guru Tom Bennett, we don't see high expectations all the time. He suggests the reason for this is that people find it uncomfortable admitting their expectations aren't high and that high expectations are subjective. He calls this 'cognitive dissonance in action' – there is a mismatch between some teachers' beliefs and actions. They claim to have high standards, but their actions say otherwise.

You establish what you establish

Bill Rogers

> YOU ESTABLISH WHAT YOU ESTABLISH

If you want punctual, hard-working and polite students, you need to show you won't tolerate anything less. You have to be clear that you will take action when your students don't uphold your high expectations. Your expectations should not be different for students who have a challenging home life, are new to your school or are on a managed move because of poor behaviour in a previous school. Sure, have short-term allowances for unexpected events, for example, a family bereavement. But long-term concessions undermine your high expectations and deprive students of learning.

Tom Bennett

> ONE OF THE BIGGEST COMPLIMENTS YOU CAN GIVE A STUDENT IS TO SAY 'I THINK YOU CAN DO IT.' WHEN YOU HAVE HIGH EXPECTATIONS, YOU TREAT THEM WITH DIGNITY, AND YOU SHOW THEM YOU CARE. (BENNETT, 2020a)

You definitely should not negotiate with naughty students and look for ways to make your job easier. It sends the message to the rest of the class that you will accept substandard work providing they are quiet. Looking the other way when a challenging student shouts out but issuing sanctions for less trivial behaviour to other students is unfair.

Establishing high expectations

The strategies in 'Strong Start', 'Establishing Routines' and 'Habits of Attention' will help you enforce and sustain high expectations. We also advise you to read Tom Bennett's

CHAPTER
CLASSROOM SYSTEMS

01 HIGH EXPECTATIONS | 02 STRONG START | 03 ESTABLISHING ROUTINES | 04 BUILDING
RELATIONSHIPS | 05 PURPOSEFUL PRAISE | 06 HABITS OF ATTENTION | 07 SEATING PLANS

Running the Room, and Tom Sherrington and Oliver Caviglioli's *Teaching WalkThrus*. Both offer a range of practical strategies to help you establish and implement high expectations.

Here are strategies we have found beneficial in helping us establish and sustain high expectations.

Be clear in what you expect

Decide your expectations and try to align these with your school's behaviour policy, vision and ethos. Your own high expectations and your school's should be mutually reinforcing. Have expectations for entering and leaving the classroom, how to listen to peers, how to ask and answer questions, and expectations around homework. Before introducing any expectations, decide what you will take a hard line on and be clear with what you want.

Never look the other way

Challenge any behaviour that falls short of your expectations. Be consistent so that you don't devalue your expectations. A good strategy for embedding your high expectations and establishing your routines is frequently checking students' understanding. Check students have understood your instructions by directing them to articulate what you have asked them to do. Doing so will help you determine if your students chose to disregard an instruction or if they didn't understand it. We advise doing this until your classes master your routines or when you need to reboot your expectations, like at the beginning of a new term.

Make explicit to students how their actions have consequences. Tom Sherrington and Oliver Caviglioli call this 'choices and consequences'. Doing so makes students responsible for making the right decision while knowing what the outcome will be if they don't. For example, 'Polly, turn and face the way you should, or you will have a break time detention.'

OBSERVE OTHER TEACHERS IN YOUR SCHOOL TO MEASURE HOW HIGH YOUR EXPECTATIONS ARE. REFLECT ON WHETHER YOU ARE ASKING TOO MUCH OR TOO LITTLE OF YOUR STUDENTS.

Tom Sherrington & Oliver Caviglioli

THE PRINCIPLE IS THAT IF STUDENTS CHOOSE TO MISBEHAVE, THEY CHOOSE TO RECEIVE THE CONSEQUENCE. (SHERRINGTON & CAVIGLIOLI, 2020)

STRONG START

A strong start to a lesson sets the foundations for purposeful learning and a calm environment.

First impressions count; don't underestimate the influence of a strong start to your lesson

Do lessons begin once your students are all in the classroom, sat down and ready to start the first activity? Or, do lessons start as your students arrive at the classroom door? Your answer to the above questions can make a difference in creating the foundations for a strong start to your lesson. For this spread, we suggest your lessons begin when students arrive at the classroom door.

SEE **SPREAD 03** TO LEARN MORE ABOUT THE IMPORTANCE OF ROUTINES.

A strong start and positive teacher–student relationships are mutually reinforcing

How you start your lesson can set the tone for how it unfolds. The ideal start is where students enter the room calmly, get ready for learning and undertake their daily review. When you establish strong-start routines, you will not have to spend as much time reinforcing them, and you can focus on taking the register. How you choose to meet and greet your students is something for you to decide, and this may depend on the expectations set out in your school. However, meeting and greeting provides opportunities for you to get to know your students and build positive relationships. It allows you to learn your students' names and to know a little more about them as individuals with a quick 'check-in' on arrival. Also, it allows you to build a routine with students assigned leadership opportunities such as handing out the exercise books.

Doug Lemov

DESIGN AND ESTABLISH AN EFFICIENT ROUTINE FOR STUDENTS TO ENTER THE CLASSROOM AND BEGIN CLASS. (LEMOV, 2021)

Strong starts maximise learning time

Ultimately, a strong start to your lesson allows you to minimise the time between students arriving at the classroom door and the lesson beginning. It will mean you can avoid unnecessary disruptions that can delay the start of your lesson, reducing the potential knock-on effect they can have on the remainder of the lesson.

CHAPTER
CLASSROOM SYSTEMS

01 HIGH EXPECTATIONS | **02 STRONG START** | 03 ESTABLISHING ROUTINES | 04 BUILDING
RELATIONSHIPS | 05 PURPOSEFUL PRAISE | 06 HABITS OF ATTENTION | 07 SEATING PLANS

HOW TO START YOUR LESSONS STRONG

Purpose and context

A strong start helps set the tone for the lesson; it builds momentum and develops academic habits. Use the following guide to build the right foundations for the beginning of every lesson.

1 Purpose and context

Be prepared for your students' arrival by having your daily review activity on the board before students enter the classroom. Also, put students' exercise books near the door for a student(s) to hand out.

2 Positive engagement

Use your students' arrival as an opportunity to interact by greeting them by their name and narrating positives. For example, acknowledge students that produced excellent work in the last lesson.

3 Reinforce expectations

Remind students of your expectations as they enter the classroom by narrating them and assigning leadership opportunities.

SPREAD

03

ESTABLISHING ROUTINES

Whether it is the start, ending or transition between
activities, routines create safe, caring and productive
learning environments.

*If you can get everyone listening whenever you
want and involve everyone in productive purposeful
talk whenever you want, you've got some basic
foundations for great lessons pretty much nailed.*

**Tom Sherrington
(2021a)**

Routines help teachers and students thrive

Routines build positive relationships, maximise learning
opportunities and reduce negative behaviour. Therefore,
you must cultivate an environment where all students feel
safe and can thrive. With a strong repertoire of routines in
your locker, you and your students will flourish.

Script, rehearse, refine and establish your routines

➕

DEVELOPED BY ADAM
BOXER, FRONT-LOADING
IS WHEN YOU PLACE
VITAL INFORMATION
AT THE BEGINNING OF
INSTRUCTION, AS THIS
IS WHEN STUDENTS
ARE MOST LIKELY TO BE
LISTENING.

Procedures become routines once they are automatic. To
establish your routines, you will need to script, rehearse
and sometimes refine them. The best teachers operate at
a high level of automaticity. A curveball like having to
distribute a previously unannounced letter will not phase
them. As an early years teacher, you might find unexpected
changes overwhelming. Having a carefully scripted
walk-through of your routines can help get you and your
students back on track.

Adam Boxer

🔊

TRY THESE FOR SIZE:
'WITHOUT TALKING, I'D
LIKE YOU TO WRITE DOWN
THREE THINGS...'

'WITHOUT CALLING OUT,
CAN ANYONE TELL ME...'

'IN SILENCE, YOU ARE
GOING TO...'
(BOXER, 2020)

Decide what you want your routines to be for the start and
end of a lesson. When scripting these, try to be terse – fewer
words will make each instruction more memorable and
easier to master. Try to front-load the key information.
Also, develop gestures and signals to complement your
verbal instructions. A simple signal might be a hand up to
signal pause or counting back from three with your fingers
when you require your students' attention.

With your routines scripted, rehearse them with your
mentor. Ask for their feedback and refine them if needed.
Rehearsing your scripted procedures will help you master
them – they will become routines. When you take your new

CHAPTER
CLASSROOM SYSTEMS

01 HIGH EXPECTATIONS | 02 STRONG START | **03 ESTABLISHING ROUTINES** | 04 BUILDING
RELATIONSHIPS | 05 PURPOSEFUL PRAISE | 06 HABITS OF ATTENTION | 07 SEATING PLANS

routines into the classroom, introduce them carefully by following your script. When you first do this, it might feel odd, but persevere so that your new procedures become the norm. Follow your routines consistently, always. Letting them slip sends the message you don't mean what you say.

Below are routines we have found very useful for different phases in lessons. Why not give some of them a go or adapt them for your own practice?

Have your 'do now' ready and meet and greet your students. Direct students to stand behind their chairs and get their equipment out. When 2/3s of the class have entered, position yourself in the centre of your classroom and signal for silence. Front-load the instructions for the do now and check students' understanding by asking a student to repeat these back to the class. Stand for one minute and 'be seen looking' – praise the students who are on-task and check in with those you suspect might not be.

START

You can, and should, use most of the routines for starting the lesson to transition between activities. Whenever you introduce a new type of activity, explicitly talk through what you expect. You will need to do this in subsequent lessons for your students to master the routine. When explaining the activity, ensure students are paying attention – direct students to sit up, look at you and have nothing in their hands. Again, front-load your instructions and ask for a student to repeat these back to the class.

TRANSITIONS

End of lesson routines help conclude your lesson in a calm and organised manner. Set homework and check that your students understand the expectations. Establish routines for packing up and returning equipment. Whatever these look like, plan for them by rehearsing, praising when students get it right or redirecting when they don't. Make sure students know the bell is a signal for you and doesn't indicate that they can leave the room. Release a few students at a time in a calm and orderly manner.

END

BUILDING RELATIONSHIPS

The teacher–student relationship is one of the most powerful levers for establishing a productive learning environment.

The gritty part

SEE **SPREAD 07** TO LEARN MORE ABOUT BEING STRATEGIC WITH SEATING PLANS

When you first start at a new school – whether it's your placement school or your first full-time role – you will be immersed in the school culture. There will be a lot to take in, and at first this might be overwhelming, but don't worry, it is normal. Give yourself time to get to know the school systems that will support you in building relationships with students. Inevitably, students will already have their favourite teacher – a teacher they get along with more than others. This doesn't mean you can't build positive relationships built on respect.

David Didau
(2018a)

When basic respect is guaranteed, relationships can flourish and schools can become the joyful communities we would all wish them to be.

Having high expectations builds trust

SEE **SPREAD 01** TO REMIND YOURSELF ABOUT HOW TO ESTABLISH HIGH EXPECTATIONS

Relationships are built on trust, respect and credibility, just like any relationship that develops during our lifetime. To build relationships, you need to begin by establishing your expectations and being consistent in how you enforce these. When there is inconsistency in how you may praise or sanction a student, relationships might break down because students will feel like they are being unfairly treated compared to their peers.

For example, Tom shouts out, and you write his name on the board as per the school behaviour system. Charlie does the same thing a few minutes later, but you don't write his name on the board. This will affect your relationship with Tom and your credibility with the rest of the teaching group.

Equally, the same applies to giving rewards. Avoid giving the same students rewards because this can affect the relationships you have with the other students in your class.

CHAPTER
CLASSROOM SYSTEMS

01 HIGH EXPECTATIONS | 02 STRONG START | 03 ESTABLISHING ROUTINES | **04 BUILDING RELATIONSHIPS** | 05 PURPOSEFUL PRAISE | 06 HABITS OF ATTENTION | 07 SEATING PLANS

You want students to believe that they all have a chance of receiving a reward as per the behaviour system.

Here's an example of what you could do to use praise to establish trust:

'At the end of the lesson today I will be rewarding people for showing excellent endeavour in their work.'

Building relationships
You will build positive relationships by having high expectations and establishing routines. Here are some additional steps you can take to help cultivate mutually respectful relationships with your students.

- Get to know your school's behaviour policy – be clear on how sanctions and rewards are applied.

- Apply the policy consistently every lesson.

- Find time to talk to students about their career flightpath outside of lessons to get to know them more.

- Use break or lunchtime as an opportunity to have these conversations.

Collaboration with colleagues
Alongside developing relationships with students, you will also be doing the same with colleagues in your department and the wider school. Use department meetings to share your expertise and look to collaboratively plan lessons and schemes of work.

SEE **SPREAD 05** TO LEARN MORE ABOUT PURPOSEFUL PRAISE

SEE **SPREAD 49** TO LEARN MORE ABOUT TEACHER INSIGHTS

PURPOSEFUL PRAISE

Use purposeful praise when students go the extra mile, not when they live up to your high expectations.

Encouragement vs praise

REFER BACK TO **SPREAD 01** TO REMIND YOURSELF ABOUT HIGH EXPECTATIONS

When students do what you expect them to do, such as getting their planners out on the desk or completing their homework on time, this should be acknowledged rather than praised. This is what you expect your students to do as part of your classroom systems. However, when students go the extra mile – above what you would normally expect – give purposeful praise. Having a clear distinction between the two will help to ensure your praise is credible.

**Doug Lemov
(2015b)**

Praise and acknowledgement should look different otherwise students will get mixed signals

A balancing act

You should carefully consider how you acknowledge and praise your students' work, effort and behaviours. There will be times when giving public acknowledgement or praise are the right things to do. However, there will also be times when this act can have the reverse effect, especially when giving praise. This is why getting to know your students is important. Over time, you will learn which students prefer public praise and who prefers private recognition. Equally, when acknowledging, you might want to be doing so more quietly. For example, if a student regularly forgets homework, avoid giving public praise. Instead, acknowledge this privately so the student knows you recognise they have met your expectations.

Giving purposeful praise

The classroom exchanges (on the right-hand side) between the teacher and a student give some examples of how you can apply a purposeful approach to giving praise.

CHAPTER
CLASSROOM SYSTEMS

01 HIGH EXPECTATIONS | 02 STRONG START | 03 ESTABLISHING ROUTINES | 04 BUILDING
RELATIONSHIPS | **05 PURPOSEFUL PRAISE** | 06 HABITS OF ATTENTION | 07 SEATING PLANS

Scenario 1 — Acknowledgement

Excellent, I can see that everyone has remembered to get their planners out.

Scenario 2 — Praise

Emma, you have demonstrated real endeavour by considering other viewpoints beyond what I'd expected on the implications of coastal management. Well done.

Scenario 3 — Acknowledgement

Jade, I'm pleased to see your homework is completed on time this week.

Scenario 4 — Praise

I've been really impressed today with the professionalism and self-awareness you have shown during our discussions about this sensitive topic.

Tom Bennett

WE KNOW THE POWER OF PRAISE TO REINFORCE STUDENTS' BEHAVIOUR AND HELP THEM UNDERSTAND WHEN THEY ARE SUCCEEDING.
(BENNETT, 2020b)

HABITS OF ATTENTION

Improving your students' habits of attention will improve their learning and help foster an inclusive learning environment where everyone feels a sense of belonging.

Zaretta Hammond

NEUROSCIENCE REMINDS US THAT BEFORE WE CAN BE MOTIVATED TO LEARN WHAT IS IN FRONT OF US, WE MUST PAY ATTENTION TO IT.

If you want your students to make academic and personal progress, direct their attention

Being intentional about developing your students' habits of attention will likely improve learning, cultivate social norms and help create an inclusive learning environment. Humans have evolved to work with and learn from others. But our attention is good at sifting out anything that doesn't match our personal motivations – multitasking is a myth. If we are serious about our students making academic and personal progress, we need to orient their focus to the things that matter most.

SEE **SPREAD 23** *TO LEARN MORE ABOUT COGNITIVE LOAD THEORY AND THE INTERACTION BETWEEN WORKING AND LONG-TERM MEMORY*

Working memory is the gatekeeper of learning

Working memory controls our attention – it is the gatekeeper to learning. You can read more about working memory on spread 23. For this spread, think of working memory as the area in our brain responsible for temporarily storing and processing information. It is limited in how much new information it can process at any given time but can be given a helping hand by our long-term memory, which is vast.

Peps Mccrea

IF WE WANT TO CONTROL WHAT OUR STUDENTS LEARN, WE'VE GOT TO BE INTENTIONAL AND SPECIFIC ABOUT WHAT THEY SHOULD BE ATTENDING TO.

Successful students don't have a larger working memory than less successful students. They don't allow their working memory to be overwhelmed by trying to process information not pertinent to the task at hand. Remember, procedures become routines when they become automatic. Any behaviour or knowledge we can call upon automatically is secure in our long-term memory. Therefore, building habits that focus our students' attention can help them manage the limitations of their working memory.

Doug Lemov's STAR is an intentional effort to direct students' attention

Habits of attention aren't exclusive to the teacher and learning materials; they should also be developed for student interactions. In an inclusive learning environment, students share answers with the rest of the class without the fear of mockery from their peers. All students feel valued and have a sense of belonging as their teacher has been intentional about directing their peers' attention. Doug Lemov's acronym, STAR, can help you develop your students' habits of attention, especially when students are verbally sharing their answers.

SIT UP — Instruct students to sit up when listening to their peers. A strong posture, and positive expression, shows students are in sync.

TRACK — To show students their voice matters, direct them to turn to face the student speaking. If the speaker sits at the front, have them turn to face the class.

APPRECIATE — Direct students to give off warm signals, such as nodding when a peer is speaking. By doing so, students gain a warm sense of acceptance.

REPHRASE — Have students rephrase the words of their peers, showing the speaker everyone was listening. Elaboration also re-exposes students to content.

Doug Lemov

... IT SEEKS TO USE THE SIGNALS PEOPLE SEND WHEN THEY ATTEND TO SOMEONE ELSE TO BUILD A STRONGER, MORE INCLUSIVE LEARNING COMMUNITY. (LEMOV, 2021)

TO BUILD STRONG ATTENTIONAL HABITS IS TO GIVE STUDENTS STEWARDSHIP OF THEIR OWN THINKING. (LEMOV, 2021)

SEATING PLANS

The positioning of your students can support effective teaching and learning.

Rachel Wannarka

Generally, teachers who want to maximise the on-task behaviour of their students during independent work should consider utilising rows rather than groups

YOUR SCHOOL MIGHT HAVE A POLICY OR EXPECTATIONS ABOUT YOUR CLASSROOM ARRANGEMENT. HERE ARE SOME REASONS – WHY, WHEREVER POSSIBLE – WE SUGGEST USING ROWS.

WHEN STUDENTS SIT IN ROWS, IT INCREASES THEIR HABITS OF CONCENTRATION.

ROWS HAVE BEEN SHOWN TO INCREASE ON-TASK BEHAVIOUR.

THE TEACHER CAN *BE SEEN LOOKING* – IT IS EASIER TO SPOT OFF-TASK STUDENTS BECAUSE THEY DON'T HAVE THEIR BACK TO THE TEACHER.

PEER INTERACTION IS STILL AN OPTION – YOU CAN DIRECT STUDENTS TO TURN TO A PARTNER IN FRONT OR BEHIND THEM WHEN NEEDED.

Planning out where you want your students to sit can help to build positive relationships and improve outcomes in the long term.

Setting the scene

In the first few weeks of starting your teaching career, you will most likely observe teachers teaching and how students interact with their teachers and peers. What you won't see is the reasons behind why students are seated where they are in the room. Seating plans are an important tool to support your lesson planning, and effective teachers use them strategically in the service of learning.

The hidden hurdles of seating plans

At the start of the academic year, teachers will take the time to decide where individual students should sit in their classroom. Getting to know the characteristics of the students you have in each teaching group is all part of being prepared. There will be times when some students have specific SENDs, meaning they will most likely be required to sit near the front of the room. Have this information to hand when you begin teaching your own groups to ensure the smoothest possible start.

Liaise with colleagues

After you have checked the specific needs of individual students, you will need to decide where to place the rest of the students. Before you do, talk to your mentor to discover more about the students. There will be colleagues in your department who have already taught them and have insights on where to best place students in the room. If we leave students to sit where they want, it can negatively

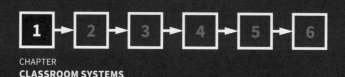

CHAPTER
CLASSROOM SYSTEMS

01 HIGH EXPECTATIONS | 02 STRONG START | 03 ESTABLISHING ROUTINES | 04 BUILDING
RELATIONSHIPS | 05 PURPOSEFUL PRAISE | 06 HABITS OF ATTENTION | **07 SEATING PLANS**

affect learning. In their 2005 study, Pace and Price found that classroom arrangement significantly impacts student behaviour.

The benefits of a seating plan and how to utilise it as part of your everyday practice

Benefit 1: Classroom ownership

When you have a seating plan prepared, it demonstrates you are in control of the lesson, which helps to build your credibility.

Benefit 2: Recalling names

It can be difficult at the beginning to recall names, but having a seating plan that is visible for you to glance at can help you to direct questions and instructions to students by using their names.

Benefit 3: Responsive teaching

Creating your seating plan means you will be looking at the characteristics of your class and the individual needs. This means you can pre-plan how you might respond during the lesson to student interactions.

Reserve front row seats for those who require more of your attention

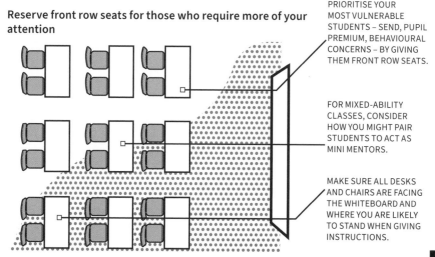

PRIORITISE YOUR MOST VULNERABLE STUDENTS – SEND, PUPIL PREMIUM, BEHAVIOURAL CONCERNS – BY GIVING THEM FRONT ROW SEATS.

FOR MIXED-ABILITY CLASSES, CONSIDER HOW YOU MIGHT PAIR STUDENTS TO ACT AS MINI MENTORS.

MAKE SURE ALL DESKS AND CHAIRS ARE FACING THE WHITEBOARD AND WHERE YOU ARE LIKELY TO STAND WHEN GIVING INSTRUCTIONS.

SUBJECT KNOWLEDGE

02

KNOWING YOUR SUBJECT

Understanding what you teach and how the content is
learned is crucial for student learning.

Creating firm foundations

There is a direct link between a teacher's subject knowledge
and their students' performance. Having secure and flexible
knowledge about your subject and how it is learned will
make you more confident and increase your students'
chances of success. Most schools you want to work at will
enquire about the strength of your subject knowledge and
your willingness to invest in nourishing it further.

The significance of deep subject knowledge is summarised
in the Great Teaching Toolkit Evidence Review.

**Deborah
Loewenberg Ball**

❞

*TEACHERS CANNOT HELP
CHILDREN LEARN THINGS
THEY THEMSELVES DO
NOT UNDERSTAND.*

'Great teachers understand the content they are teaching
and how it is learnt. This means teachers should have deep
and fluent knowledge and flexible understanding of the
content they are teaching and how it is learnt.'

Knowing your subject is the first step, and the final part
of the quote is significant because there is a difference
between subject knowledge and how to teach it to create
the right conditions for students to learn. It is normal when
you start teaching not to know everything about your
subject because there will be parts of the curriculum you
will not have studied in depth at university. The first step
to building deep and fluent knowledge of your subject is
to acknowledge this and consider how you can utilise the
expertise of colleagues within your department. Equally,
you will bring your expertise that other colleagues will
learn and benefit from through collaborative curriculum
conversations. Subject knowledge can be as much a silver
bullet as an Achilles heel.

Striking the right balance

While your subject knowledge is an important pillar
for successful teaching, there is a side to expertise that
can create a hurdle: the curse of knowledge. The curse
of knowledge is when someone who is an expert in their
field forgets other people's knowledge bases, which can

CHAPTER
SUBJECT KNOWLEDGE

08 KNOWING YOUR SUBJECT | 09 ENGLISH | 10 MATHS | 11 SCIENCE | 12 GEOGRAPHY | 13 HISTORY |
14 RELIGIOUS EDUCATION | 15 ART | 16 MUSIC | 17 PHYSICAL EDUCATION | 18 DESIGN & TECHNOLOGY |
19 COMPUTER SCIENCE | 20 BUSINESS & ECONOMICS | 21 DRAMA | 22 DANCE |

be a common pitfall of teachers. It is easy for teachers to overlook students' starting points, assuming they know something because we do or because it has been taught by someone else.

When planning your lessons, having this awareness of your own knowledge of the content to be taught and students' prior knowledge will enhance your practice. It will allow you to seek out support from colleagues in your department and decide how you will check students' prior knowledge before introducing new content for them to learn.

The diagram below, by Efrat Furst, depicts the construction of knowledge. Knowledge is represented by triangles that accumulate, connect and build up to create a pyramid. Notice how the novice pyramid shows a fewer number of triangles; it is narrower and less tall? The expert pyramid is broad, tall and made up of more triangles. It shows how knowledge begets knowledge and how what we know determines what we can know. Having secure knowledge about a subject isn't just about knowing a lot of stuff about that domain; you need to know how to sequence concepts effectively, chunk them into small chunks and much more.

Dr Niki Kaiser

ALL TEACHERS ARE EXPERTS WITH A HIGH DEGREE OF SUBJECT KNOWLEDGE, BUT WHAT MAKES US DIFFERENT ... IS OUR ABILITY TO UNDERSTAND HOW TO SUPPORT STUDENTS TO BUILD UNDERSTANDING AND EXPERTISE.

DIAGRAM USED WITH PERMISSION FROM EFRAT FURST

Introducing the subjects
On the following spreads, you will find experts in their subjects offering top tips and best bets from their respective disciplines. While most of the contributions are from secondary practitioners, we think you will find them helpful no matter your phase.

ENGLISH

Archaic writing like Shakespeare can be daunting. Guiding students through the process will unlock meaning.

Jade Hickin
Trust-wide lead
practitioner in
English

The challenge of archaic texts

Tackling passages containing archaic language can be one of the most daunting experiences for students in English. The challenge of texts that contain both out-of-use vocabulary and syntax has been highlighted by researchers such as Lemov. We need to use scaffolds to approach texts of high complexity, such as Shakespeare, so that students can engage with meaning and feel a sense of accomplishment.

You are the expert

You are the expert in the room and your skilled expert knowledge of the passage is key in developing the understanding. This means that it is important that you know the context, language and interpretations in depth prior to delivering the lesson. Do your research, annotate your copy of the text, and make sure you know more than just the scope of this lesson.

Doug Lemov

WITH EACH PASSING YEAR, ARCHAIC TEXTS BECOME A LITTLE LESS FAMILIAR AND A LITTLE MORE DISTANT FROM THE WAY WE WRITE AND TALK TODAY.
(LEMOV, 2021)

The sequence you use in teaching this passage will also need to be carefully planned and practised in order to maximise student participation and thought, while allowing for a high success rate and therefore confidence in the class. You are the best reader in that classroom. Practise reading the passage aloud to yourself so that you are not doing it for the first time in front of the class. Look up pronunciations of unfamiliar words as well as their definitions to provide students with them.

Units of meaning

Make sure you break the text into manageable chunks. A unit of meaning could be a sentence or two that are focused on conveying one complete idea. Showing students how to do this is particularly important when dealing with texts written in prose. After breaking down a passage like this, make sure that you put it back together again and consolidate understanding using comprehension questions with which you can check for understanding.

CHAPTER
SUBJECT KNOWLEDGE

08 KNOWING YOUR SUBJECT | **09 ENGLISH** | 10 MATHS | 11 SCIENCE | 12 GEOGRAPHY | 13 HISTORY |
14 RELIGIOUS EDUCATION | 15 ART | 16 MUSIC | 17 PHYSICAL EDUCATION | 18 DESIGN & TECHNOLOGY |
19 COMPUTER SCIENCE | 20 BUSINESS & ECONOMICS | 21 DRAMA | 22 DANCE |

Reassure and model

Reassure your students that they are
not expected to understand all of the
language and meaning straight away.
Read the passage aloud to your students.
Your pronunciation and prosody will
start to convey the meanings, emotions
and ideas.

Break it down

Break the passage down into sections of one or two
sentences that you see as units of meaning. Model dividing
the text into these under a visualiser so students can follow
you. Provide the students with simple definitions for the
most complex vocabulary in the passage. Use synonyms in
their most concise form to reduce cognitive load. Again,
model this under a visualiser.

Doug Lemov

*ACCESSING THESE TEXTS
IS INTEGRAL TO BECOMING
AN ENGAGED CITIZEN OF
THE WORLD.
(LEMOV, 2015b)*

Question – Read – Question

Take each unit of meaning individually. Use direct
questions to guide students in developing their
understanding. For example, 'Who is the character
speaking to here?' or 'How does the speaker feel here?'
Read the unit aloud again before taking responses through
mini whiteboards or Cold Calling. For more challenging
units, ask students to engage in a 30 second turn and talk to
rehearse their responses. When all units of meaning have
been unlocked, read the
whole passage through
again. Now you can
give students individual
comprehension questions
to consolidate and check
for their understanding.

*How does the
speaker feel
here?*

SPREAD

10

MATHS

Mathematical misconceptions are commonplace –
understanding how and why they arise is critical.

Simon Cox
Director of Blackpool
Research School

Subject knowledge matters!

We know that the most effective teachers have deep knowledge of the subjects they teach. Mathematics is a subject rife with student misconceptions, and a lack of our own understanding of mathematical concepts can exacerbate these.

Reading about mathematics can be tricky, but there are ways in which you can refresh and update your understanding. Subject associations (such as the MA and ATM) offer reduced membership for ECTs, with access to their high-quality journals. Maths Hubs offer subject knowledge enhancement, as do many other PD providers. But one of the richest resources is right in front of you: your fellow teachers. Pop into lessons, chat about upcoming topics you need support with and don't be afraid to ask for help.

Peter Henderson
(EEF, 2017)

Teachers with knowledge of common misconceptions can plan lessons to address potential misconceptions before they arise

But it's not just subject knowledge that matters. An understanding of likely misconceptions students might develop is vital, but we often only develop this over time. Remember: the ECF highlights the importance of 'working closely with colleagues to develop an understanding of likely misconceptions' and you should take frequent opportunities to discuss upcoming topics with them and others. You can then use this knowledge to confront student misconceptions head on.

1 → 2 → 3 → 4 → 5 → 6

CHAPTER
SUBJECT KNOWLEDGE

08 KNOWING YOUR SUBJECT | 09 ENGLISH | **10 MATHS** | 11 SCIENCE | 12 GEOGRAPHY | 13 HISTORY |
14 RELIGIOUS EDUCATION | 15 ART | 16 MUSIC | 17 PHYSICAL EDUCATION | 18 DESIGN & TECHNOLOGY |
19 COMPUTER SCIENCE | 20 BUSINESS & ECONOMICS | 21 DRAMA | 22 DANCE |

Minimising misconceptions
Using your knowledge to confront issues head on.

Research common misconceptions
Seek out published sources of common misconceptions, and discuss these in meetings with your mentor. How could you assess any existing misconceptions students might hold – for example, using multiple choice questions?

Explore why they persist
At which point in the learning journey has a misconception arisen? Providing convincing counter-examples can help: for example, using a bar diagram to convince a student who incorrectly adds the numerators and denominators when adding fractions.

Address the misconceptions
Is there opportunity to collaborate as a team, possibly through discussion of common misconceptions in team meetings?

Consider possible future issues
The language we use in the classroom is of particular importance, and avoiding problematic phrases or unhelpful shortcuts – even if they seem useful at the time – could minimise the development of future misconceptions. So avoid saying 'multiplication makes bigger' – even if it does for the numbers you are using.

Plan tasks that can help
Provide examples and non-examples of concepts, discuss and compare different solution approaches, use multiple choice questions with plausible distractors, and provide opportunities for students to investigate mathematical structure and make generalisations.

SPREAD

11

SCIENCE

Science is a massive and rewarding discipline.
Follow strategies for excellent planning, execution
and augmentation of content.

Jo Castelino
Second in science
and teaching and
learning lead

Teaching science involves knowledge of the subject but more importantly how to explain it

Science is a fascinating subject to teach. When done well, students will enthuse about concepts learned in lessons, start to make sense of things happening around them and appreciate the value and effort that went into the development of ideas over the years.

To get students to this stage, first we need to plan our explanations and hinterland (the stories that support and augment the core knowledge).

Most science teachers are specialists in one of the three main sciences, but in most schools teachers will have to teach a science that is outside their specialism. This can seem daunting at first.

Focus on improving explanations, models (such as worked examples), checks for understanding and practice questions as these will have the greatest impact on student learning.

Think of lessons as a teaching sequence rather than an hour-long session.

When designing a teaching sequence, think about the key parts of a concept and have an idea of the content students have already learned and what content is still to come.

One key aspect of knowing your subject is discussion with experienced and specialist teachers. Look at their resources, talk to them at length about planning teaching sequences, designing explanations and checking for understanding. These specialist teachers may be in your department or in other schools. EduTwitter is also a brilliant place to share and discuss ideas.

CHAPTER
SUBJECT KNOWLEDGE

08 KNOWING YOUR SUBJECT | 09 ENGLISH | 10 MATHS | **11 SCIENCE** | 12 GEOGRAPHY | 13 HISTORY |
14 RELIGIOUS EDUCATION | 15 ART | 16 MUSIC | 17 PHYSICAL EDUCATION | 18 DESIGN & TECHNOLOGY |
19 COMPUTER SCIENCE | 20 BUSINESS & ECONOMICS | 21 DRAMA | 22 DANCE |

How to plan your teaching sequences

Write a list of core questions. Use the national curriculum, textbooks, revision guides and resources used by specialist teachers to inform your list. The **CogSciSci** website is a great place to find resources such as Retrieval Roulette (an Excel file with core questions) and booklets.

SEE **SPREAD 28** TO LEARN MORE ABOUT RETRIEVAL PRACTICE

Know the sequence of lessons and identify the foundational knowledge that needs to be secure before new content is introduced.

SEE **SPREAD 34** TO LEARN MORE ABOUT CURRICULUM KNOWLEDGE

Discuss your teaching sequence with a specialist teacher.

Decide how you will present and explain the core concepts within your teaching sequence.

SEE **SPREAD 23** TO LEARN MORE ABOUT COGNITIVE LOAD THEORY

Think about reducing extraneous cognitive load by directing student attention on one thing at a time.

Decide on examples, non-examples and boundary examples to clarify a concept.

COGSCISCI: HTTPS:// COGSCISCI. WORDPRESS.COM/ RESOURCES/

Know the hinterland that can support and augment your teaching of the core content. Some science hinterland stories can be found at #ScienceStories, collated by Bill Wilkinson.

#SCIENCESTORIES: https://drive.google. com/drive/u/0/mobile/ folders/1E4DmRaHYCQ 7XkoatL-koV7VPHIZu06 Y0?usp=drive_open

Identify potential misconceptions. These can be found in examiner reports for past exam questions or by discussing them with experienced colleagues.

ADAM BOXER'S BOOK: TEACHING SECONDARY SCIENCE: A COMPLETE GUIDE

Plan to explicitly make links between content so students can build schemas. This is crucial to help students understand teaching sequences and not just see units of content as discrete entities.

SPREAD

12

GEOGRAPHY

Knowing your subject is important, but knowing what is important is key.

Laura Pellegrino
Team leader for KS3 geography

The power of subject knowledge is transformative within every aspect of teaching, but runs the risk of being overwhelming

On day one of my teacher training I was handed a 10-page document in size 8 font; a subject knowledge audit. As a human geographer, my stomach fell as I scored myself low on the physical aspects of the audit. Even more so by the end of the course, where for many of those aspects, I still lacked any substantive knowledge. For many early career and experienced teachers, subject knowledge is a silent catalyst of imposter syndrome that can commandeer the joy of teaching.

Confidence stems from preparation

There's a saying that floats around the teaching profession that you 'only have to be a page ahead of the students', and while this may sound comforting, it in reality only adds to the issue. Why? Because you live in a perpetual state of not knowing what is next, which ultimately stops students from being able to access bigger-picture thinking. A great place to start is creating an open dialogue with your department to help understand your subject's curriculum journey; the what, the why and the why now.

Understanding the knowledge you need

Geography as a subject, for example, is interdisciplinary by nature and the scope of potential knowledge is infinite, so it is important to understand the core knowledge and separate it from the anecdotal. Starting at the end with the intended learning outcome – whether that is from schemes of work, specifications or the national curriculum – will put you in a strong position. Dedicate a time slot in your week for reading and making basic notes on topics, to refer to in lessons if needed. This will not only provide an extra layer of comfort, but is a prime opportunity to think about questioning and checking for understanding activities.

CHAPTER
SUBJECT KNOWLEDGE

08 KNOWING YOUR SUBJECT | 09 ENGLISH | 10 MATHS | 11 SCIENCE | **12 GEOGRAPHY** | 13 HISTORY |
14 RELIGIOUS EDUCATION | 15 ART | 16 MUSIC | 17 PHYSICAL EDUCATION | 18 DESIGN & TECHNOLOGY |
19 COMPUTER SCIENCE | 20 BUSINESS & ECONOMICS | 21 DRAMA | 22 DANCE |

Subject knowledge is not just the what, but the how

Knowing the formation of a meander is one thing, but teaching it to students is another. Utilise examiner reports and mark schemes to see how answers could be presented in a formal setting, or observe/role play the teaching of the concept with a member of your department prior to delivering to students.

Teamwork makes the dream work

Yes, you have your teaching load and classes you are responsible for, but you work as part of a team: use them! As a human geographer, I'll be the first to admit that I do not share the depth of knowledge or enthusiasm for some aspects of the physical side of geography as my colleagues. Instead of dwelling on knowledge shortfalls, utilise the specialisms within your department by partaking in team teaching, one-to-one CPD or observing best practice (unfortunately for my department I'm still not a fan of rocks).

Embrace a 'no error' culture

This is the most crucial point; we are human. We all make mistakes. Whether you are in your first year or thirty-first year of teaching, we get things wrong, or the art of articulation is momentarily lost. Model and embrace the ups and downs of learning to your students; they'll appreciate it, and it takes alleviates pressure you didn't know was on your shoulders.

Platforms to explore for subject knowledge enhancement:

Department curriculum documents	Subject associations (e.g. the GA/RGS) through conferences, lectures, CPD courses	Observing best practice (in your department and across other schools)
Exam board specifications/ examiners reports/ textbooks	TeachMeets e.g. researchED	Social media (e.g. #geographyteacher on Twitter)

SPREAD

13

HISTORY

This spread offers a practical guide to help you upskill your subject knowledge in history.

Rebecca Chadwick
Lead practitioner of history

It's okay not to know everything!

As a first year teacher, it is easy to fall into the trap of trying to convince your students that you know everything. However, this is normally not the case. Before you begin your first teaching role, look at the schemes of work and exam board for your department. Use these to rate your subject knowledge in each area before you begin.

How to close your knowledge gaps

Consult your department first: is there an expert in a particular area of history, or someone who has taught the exam board for years? Speak to them and ask for the key elements students need to know to succeed in the module. For GCSE and A-level, focus on the textbook as your starting point as this should contain the key information that your students need to know and read around this. Use books such as the *A Brief History of…* or the *Penguin Monarchs* series as a quick win to help subject knowledge.

Read, read and read some more

I am an avid reader, making this piece of advice easier for me, but I strongly believe that one of the greatest elements of being a history teacher is the stories of the past. Read around your subject – a quick Twitter search will probably guide you to which books. This will not only help you to be constantly learning and upskilling your subject knowledge, but it will provide you with additional stories and anecdotes to tell the students and ignite their passion beyond the specification.

CHAPTER
SUBJECT KNOWLEDGE

08 KNOWING YOUR SUBJECT | 09 ENGLISH | 10 MATHS | 11 SCIENCE | 12 GEOGRAPHY | **13 HISTORY** |
14 RELIGIOUS EDUCATION | 15 ART | 16 MUSIC | 17 PHYSICAL EDUCATION | 18 DESIGN & TECHNOLOGY |
19 COMPUTER SCIENCE | 20 BUSINESS & ECONOMICS | 21 DRAMA | 22 DANCE |

> *Let your passion for history shine through your lessons, making students understand the significance of the content.*

Confidence in your subject knowledge brings confidence in your teaching

Knowing your subject helps to make you feel more confident in your teaching and will help you to be able to plan more effective lessons. By having the confidence in dates, figures, people and events relating to the area of history, this will help you to develop your questioning and produce resources to fit the knowledge. I find that the areas of history that my subject knowledge is weakest in, are often some of my best lessons, as I have seen from a learner's perspective the difficult areas and concepts of the topic.

Investigate and modify

Speak to your department and find out if they have subscriptions to Teaching History or the Historical Association. These are ways of getting short articles that will help to build your subject knowledge, and they often provide scholarship and interpretations, which you can then use in your classroom and resourcing. Use social media such as the History Teacher Book Club on Twitter, who read and discuss many new books related to key topics in history each half-term. They have also started to provide Zoom conversations with the authors, giving us key quotes that we can take into our classrooms the very next day.

SPREAD

14

RELIGIOUS EDUCATION

The nature and purpose of RE is contested. Make sure you are clear about this in your teaching.

Dawn Cox
Head of RE

What is RE?

This might seem to be an odd way to start a section on religious education. Throughout its history, RE has had various incarnations and continues to vary in practice between teachers and between schools.

There is a current push for change that involves a shift in how it is taught and what should be taught as part of the curriculum. Known as the religion and worldviews paradigm, it aims to reflect 'the complex, diverse and plural nature of religious and non-religious worldviews'.

RELIGION AND WORLDVIEWS IS A NEW WAY OF THINKING ABOUT WHAT ROLE RE PLAYS IN THE CURRICULUM

Types of knowledge

One way that the Ofsted RE research review approaches curriculum progression is through *types of knowledge*. These three different types of knowledge allow us to focus specifically on what it is that our students are getting better at in RE.

THE 2021 OFSTED RESEARCH REVIEW IS AN EXCELLENT SOURCE ON HIGH-QUALITY RE

Substantive knowledge is the content that we teach students about religious and non-religious traditions, the selection of which will depend on the syllabus your school follows. There can be some freedom for schools to choose what substantive knowledge they want to teach. It should be carefully thought about in terms of school context, prior and post key stages, and the sequencing of knowledge which builds up to create a schema. As we often have little curriculum time, our rationale and decision making on content selection needs to be clear.

ALL STATE-FUNDED SCHOOLS AND ACADEMIES IN ENGLAND MUST PROVIDE RE TO ALL CHILDREN ON THE SCHOOL ROLL

Ofsted call the second type of knowledge *ways of knowing* but it can also be referred to as *disciplinary knowledge*. This is the ways in which we can study the substantive knowledge; the methods and the tools we can use. Some teachers use theology, philosophy and social sciences but there is some debate within the community as to what else should be included and what these disciplines include. Some teachers use one discipline to approach a topic and some will use more than one.

CHAPTER
SUBJECT KNOWLEDGE

08 KNOWING YOUR SUBJECT | 09 ENGLISH | 10 MATHS | 11 SCIENCE | 12 GEOGRAPHY | 13 HISTORY |
14 RELIGIOUS EDUCATION | 15 ART | 16 MUSIC | 17 PHYSICAL EDUCATION | 18 DESIGN & TECHNOLOGY |
19 COMPUTER SCIENCE | 20 BUSINESS & ECONOMICS | 21 DRAMA | 22 DANCE |

The third way of knowing is *personal knowledge* or a *personal worldview*. This idea suggests that our students should understand that their own views are not neutral and that they are influenced by many things over their lifetime that contribute to their worldview. The purpose of RE is for students to realise this concept of a personal view and acknowledge that it can change over time. Some have used the metaphor of a lens to help students understand how this works.

We can plan our curriculum and lessons to include these types of knowledge over time and to develop student knowledge and understanding while practising using the disciplines using a variety of religious and non-religious views.

Example of using the disciplines

Topic: The Fall

Theology – What might the Fall show Christians about the relationship between God and humans?

Philosophy – Do humans really have free will?

Social sciences – Do all Christians believe the Fall actually happened? How can we find out?

Conceptual golden threads

Another way of pulling together your RE lessons is to develop *threads* using substantive conceptual knowledge. If we carefully consider what these might be in what we're teaching we can emphasise them and then refer to them at a later date to compare and contrast depending on the context. For example, the concept of prayer goes across religions but there are differences between them in its significance and how it is practised. Once students understand this concept they may apply it in future contexts and have something to add to their existing schema of prayer. By using substantive concepts we can teach commonality and diversity in religious and non-religious beliefs.

CONCEPTS IN RE:

1 – THOSE COMMON TO ALL HUMANS

2 – THOSE THAT GO ACROSS RELIGIONS

3 – THOSE THAT ARE UNIQUE TO A CERTAIN RELIGION

ART

Art is a wonderful subject. It is vast, varied, creative and exciting.

Jo Baker
Assistant principal
and art teacher

Art teachers come from a huge range of specialisms; you will find that no two art departments are the same. This is what makes them exciting. Get to know the specialisms within your team. Departments work with these specialisms at the core of everything they do.

Curriculum

Focus on the curriculum in your department. Make sure you teach the skills well in KS3. Focus on developing artists from day one. Ensure your curriculum develops students' skill as well as their creative exploration. You cannot have one without the other.

Be the expert

Teach correct skill and technique early, in order to allow students to explore creatively later on. Students need to know how to use media, techniques and processes well in order to manage them effectively. Show students the correct technique. Give effective, confident and skilful demonstrations. You are the master craftsman, the students your apprentices. Equip them with the tools, and then allow them to explore and get creative. Encourage students to explore and hone the techniques. The best bit about being an art teacher is that you are learning and developing too! A lack of knowledge and skill can lead to frustration later down the line. If a technique is new to you, tell the students. Learn together. Discuss the best way forward. Share ideas. You cannot know everything. Art is too broad to know everything.

Be encouraging

Art is daunting. Everything a student creates is instantly on show. Art can make students feel vulnerable. Be encouraging and build up their confidence. This is my number one rule. Create a no-fear classroom. High challenge, low threat.

CHAPTER
SUBJECT KNOWLEDGE

08 KNOWING YOUR SUBJECT | 09 ENGLISH | 10 MATHS | 11 SCIENCE | 12 GEOGRAPHY | 13 HISTORY |
14 RELIGIOUS EDUCATION | **15 ART** | 16 MUSIC | 17 PHYSICAL EDUCATION | 18 DESIGN & TECHNOLOGY |
19 COMPUTER SCIENCE | 20 BUSINESS & ECONOMICS | 21 DRAMA | 22 DANCE |

Be enthusiastic

Be the students' cheerleader. Encourage and build their confidence. Art students need to feel nurtured. It is important students feel safe to explore.

Be brave

Get comfortable with not knowing everything. Be comfortable with students being better than you. There are always students who amaze us – be encouraged by them. In these circumstances you become more coach than instructor.

Be broad

Explore a wide range of media and techniques in your curriculum. I have found that everyone excels in something; you need to give all students a chance to succeed. Introducing your students to a wide range of media and techniques will give you a huge variety of outcomes later on.

Art as a subject is vast. Art is all around us, and has a varied and rich history. There will never come a time when you know everything, so be okay with exploring alongside your students. Foster a sense of creative exploration in your classroom. Students need to know that it is okay to not be immediately successful. Create resilient, curious students who explore and experiment to get the best results. A creative confidence is at the heart of every amazing art classroom.

Learn from your students. Keep creating yourself.

Build students' skills alongside their confidence. Watch their creativity soar.

SPREAD

16

MUSIC
Singing can be the most important part of a child's week.
Here is how to prepare!

Nicholas Sermon
Primary phase
class teacher and
music lead

As a new teacher, the opportunities that singing provides are unique

Singing promotes discipline and teamwork, skills that are vital for a child's development, and has a positive impact on the mental wellbeing of everyone involved. Before starting to sing, prepare the children first by thinking about their posture. A good posture supports a stronger, more confident singer in the long term.

Warm up the voice as you would a muscle, with a task that will ensure that no one damages their vocal cords. It should promote good breathing. The warm-up doesn't need to be complicated (in fact, the simpler, the better). Breathing deeply and focusing on producing a hum is effective.

Select music that you enjoy! If you are going to join the class, make sure it's a piece that you feel confident in supporting. It's likely that a good proportion of the children won't have heard the music, so introducing this to them will broaden their knowledge of the piece. Spend some time talking about the piece and sharing thoughts collectively with the children. This will prove to be even more powerful if there's a performance you can share with others. Play this to the class as it will contextualise the performance.

Focus on the starting note and the last note of the piece. This allows the class to know how to effectively move around the piece. Don't worry if it doesn't sound great to start; constant repetition will build up awareness of the piece. Remember to sing with your class. No child will judge what you sound like. If you go wrong, enjoy the moment of laughter it will bring.

Singing is important for wellbeing

Singing has been shown to make people more positive than if they passively listen. Take time to incorporate singing into your week, and the children will love the moment that they get to work as a team.

CHAPTER
SUBJECT KNOWLEDGE

08 KNOWING YOUR SUBJECT | 09 ENGLISH | 10 MATHS | 11 SCIENCE | 12 GEOGRAPHY | 13 HISTORY |
14 RELIGIOUS EDUCATION | 15 ART | **16 MUSIC** | 17 PHYSICAL EDUCATION | 18 DESIGN & TECHNOLOGY |
19 COMPUTER SCIENCE | 20 BUSINESS & ECONOMICS | 21 DRAMA | 22 DANCE |

HOW TO GET YOUR CLASS TO SING

Purpose and context

Approach the opportunity ensuring that you follow a clear structure to the task. By doing this, the process will become smooth and everyone will enjoy the experience.

1 Good posture

Make sure that students all have enough room and demonstrate how they should stand. Feet shoulder-width apart and the body should be relaxed.

Your feet should be shoulder-width apart

2 Warm up

Start off with a simple warm up. Humming up and down a scale is a good starting point. However, you can find many examples on the internet that are excellent. Experiment with different types to motivate your class.

3 Music

Make sure that it's a piece that you enjoy! Share this with the class. Sing and enjoy. Breakdown by identifying simple points, like the start and end note. Don't be afraid to write it on the music.

SPREAD

17

PHYSICAL EDUCATION

Revisit previously learned content to embed learning in seemingly separate current topics.

David Morgan
PE curriculum leader

UNDERSTAND THE REASON FOR CURRICULUM SEQUENCING, THEN LOOK FOR KNOWLEDGE THREAD OPPORTUNITIES.

Rotation-based curriculum models should not restrict interleaving opportunities

Certain subject areas choose to follow a rotational curriculum model. This involves students spending a set amount of time on a topic area, then moving on to a different aspect of their curriculum (e.g. continuing with your current class or class moves to next teacher). Reasons for these models can be the reality of teaching practical-based subjects, with factors affecting our choice of curriculum sequencing ranging from available facilities, staff specialisms or even the weather. So how do we ensure that we can weave in previously learned content, to strengthen learning in seemingly independent topic areas?

Interleaving principles can maximise learning and increase retrieval opportunities

Unlike 'static' classroom-based subjects, where content sequencing is very clear, we have to look for transferable skills that could or should be used to help knowledge retention of present content. It is this strategic weaving of knowledge that will allow students to see the big picture of your overall intent, allowing staff to observe student understanding as they navigate through the curriculum.

Tactical 'knowledge threads' and when to weave them

Your current lessons do not have to be littered with these interleaving opportunities. They should be carefully considered during the unit of work that allows them to make strong connections in learning. You may be faced with consecutive topics such as: gymnastics to football, food and nutrition to product design, music technology to group performances (playing instruments). Be tactical in how you interleave; it must be beneficial to building schema.

CHAPTER
SUBJECT KNOWLEDGE

08 KNOWING YOUR SUBJECT | 09 ENGLISH | 10 MATHS | 11 SCIENCE | 12 GEOGRAPHY | 13 HISTORY |
14 RELIGIOUS EDUCATION | 15 ART | 16 MUSIC | **17 PHYSICAL EDUCATION** | 18 DESIGN & TECHNOLOGY |
19 COMPUTER SCIENCE | 20 BUSINESS & ECONOMICS | 21 DRAMA | 22 DANCE |

HOW TO WEAVE KNOWLEDGE THREADS

Purpose and context

Revisiting previously learned material can encourage understanding by allowing us to make memory associations from our prior knowledge.

1   What are your threads?

Look at your curriculum maps and schemes of work, and speak with your department to identify topic aspects that can become knowledge threads. Shoehorned threads are no good to anyone; they will just confuse students.

2   When will you weave?

Have an idea of your unit delivery and plan where and when the interleaving opportunities should take place.
They need to complement the current learning.

3   How will you know it's worked?

Check for understanding to review the effectiveness of the knowledge threads. Use a variety of methods like practical performances, questions and answers, dialogue and discussions.

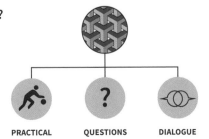

PRACTICAL   QUESTIONS   DIALOGUE

DESIGN & TECHNOLOGY

Make it, don't fake it. It's important to understand and grasp what students will be learning.

Drew Wicken
Director of design and technology

It's vital to understand what students will be learning in your lessons

To ensure that you really understand what your department's curriculum design offers its students, you must make what you are teaching. It sounds simple enough. However, it is something that many teachers don't do, leading to a breakdown in the core knowledge and skills being taught.

Take the time to understand the highs and lows of the learning being completed

By undertaking the work students will be tasked with in your lessons, it will give you a clearer idea as to where the pitfalls and challenges arise during the work. By getting a strong grasp of what will be manufactured, cooked or designed, it will give you confidence when in front of the students. This will only enhance your opportunities to get students passionate about the learning and achieve some high-quality outcomes. Furthermore, it will give you the ability to adapt and scaffold the learning for the students you are teaching.

Modelling the work can support all of your learners to achieve

Further to giving you a better understanding of the learning being completed, it will also give you worked examples of the learning being completed. By displaying examples of learning needed to be completed, it can demonstrate to students what needs to be achieved in the kitchen, workshop or design studio.

Oracy in D&T

Throughout our subject, there are hundreds of key terms and concepts that require students to understand and grasp them to be able to fully access the learning. Making sure students understand these key terms and concepts will unlock their potential to heighten their abilities to design and manufacture in D&T.

CHAPTER
SUBJECT KNOWLEDGE

08 KNOWING YOUR SUBJECT | 09 ENGLISH | 10 MATHS | 11 SCIENCE | 12 GEOGRAPHY | 13 HISTORY |
14 RELIGIOUS EDUCATION | 15 ART | 16 MUSIC | 17 PHYSICAL EDUCATION | **18 DESIGN & TECHNOLOGY** |
19 COMPUTER SCIENCE | 20 BUSINESS & ECONOMICS | 21 DRAMA | 22 DANCE |

Talk like a designer

The Education Endowment Foundation (EEF, 2018c) discuss how, when students can access the powerful words in a given subject, they can add as much as six months to their learning in a year. Therefore it is vital that, within D&T, we are equipping our students with the knowledge and understanding so that they can use these key terms in their classwork. This will ensure that students can articulate themselves in a professional manner, allowing them to demonstrate the learning within a given topic.

If we restrict students' access to the powerful terms within our subject we are instantly creating a barrier to their learning. Therefore, be unashamedly proud of teaching your students the key terms and concepts in D&T. However, it is important not only that they learn to spell these words, but also grasp the meaning and etymological routes of those powerful terms. Here are some great opportunities to ensure that literacy is built into your D&T lessons.

Recipes are great ways to convey key information. Allowing students to read, highlight and question what is happening in the recipe will give you a clear understanding as to what they understand and where there are gaps.

Students should also read aloud the design context and discuss with other students what they believe the task is going to require of them. This will give them an opportunity to discuss the design skills that will be required. Moreover, you can ensure that key terms are written into the design context for them to fully grasp what they mean.

When evaluating the work undertaken, get students into threes, where they can critically reflect on each others work. During the discussion, give students a crib sheet of key terms and concepts you want them to discuss. This will ensure that students are using those powerful words in discussions with other students.

COMPUTER SCIENCE

Computer science is a subject fraught with misconceptions –
use PRIMM to address them head-on.

Karl McGrath
Year 5 teacher and
task design
and curriculum
implementation lead

PRIMM STANDS
FOR PREDICT, RUN,
INVESTIGATE, MODIFY,
AND MAKE.

DEVELOPED BY SUE
SENTANCE, THIS
APPROACH IS USED
TO TEACH CODE TO
INTERNALISE A WORKED
EXAMPLE PRIOR TO
STUDENTS CREATING
THEIR OWN.

Learning code is like learning a new language

What is your first step when teaching students how to code?
Do you explicitly show or tell them what to input line by
line? Do you hand them a sheet to copy code from and hope
that enough of them can do it to pull the rest along? If the
answer is yes to any of these, then for this spread I would
suggest adopting the PRIMM approach.

Often when teaching or demonstrating a process, we will allow the children to generate ideas first

It is important students understand the purpose of code
and importantly the syntax. Code is a language and within
that language exist 'dialects'. For example, children can be
taught to code in Python, Java or C++ and there are subtle
differences in each of these. Firstly, it's important to start
by exploring the language at hand. PRIMM is taught in
phases and it's important to note there's no set timetable
to these. With PRIMM you are involving the children in
the modelling process, as you are actively encouraging
the children to investigate and modify a worked example,
much like how we encourage children to investigate and
internalise texts to write their own in a specific style.

PRIMM is a powerful scaffold offering highly specific tasks to complete

Using PRIMM in your computer science lessons allows you
to structure the sequence of lessons in a way that guides the
learner through the process to understanding. This is not
only useful for novice learners, but can provide invaluable
support for all learners in what can be a particularly
difficult process.

It's important to note that this is how I use this technique,
and while I may suggest combining one or more elements,
this is due to my experience with my learners.

CHAPTER
SUBJECT KNOWLEDGE

08 KNOWING YOUR SUBJECT | 09 ENGLISH | 10 MATHS | 11 SCIENCE | 12 GEOGRAPHY | 13 HISTORY |
14 RELIGIOUS EDUCATION | 15 ART | 16 MUSIC | 17 PHYSICAL EDUCATION | 18 DESIGN & TECHNOLOGY |
19 COMPUTER SCIENCE | 20 BUSINESS & ECONOMICS | 21 DRAMA | 22 DANCE |

Predict and run

First, you need to show students an extract of code in pseudocode, block form or written. I recommend something short that can be interpreted for discussion and, ultimately, prediction. After children discuss and generate ideas then you would allow time to share. Next, you run the code, asking questions like, 'Did the code behave in the way you expected? Why not?'

```
<p>Save the document
by pressing <kbd>Ctrl +
S</kbd></p>
```

Investigate and modify

Here is your chance to explore the code either by piece, block or line by line. Ensure you ask questions to check for understanding, such as, 'What would happen if I changed this number? Is there a way to make this line simpler or more effective?' Once you and the students have investigated and unpicked the code, you can either allow them to copy it to the code to make something themselves or you can give them another similar example. The purpose here is simple; a blank page can be very daunting, and this way the children have a worked example to build on.

Make

This is the moment where the students get the opportunity to write their own program based on the worked example or examples shared as a class. The key thing is to encourage changes and amendments to the original. I always liken it to other colleagues to Pie Corbett's innovation of an internalised text.

Sarah Jones
Subject leader for business, economics and finance

Encouraging students to bring information to mind regularly is the key to securing basic knowledge

Recreate to automate. This is my mantra. In order to develop fluency with key concepts, provide students with plenty of retrieval practice opportunities. Examples could include a finance sources definition quiz, a blank paper 'brain dump' on types of growth, or a cost curve drawing challenge on mini whiteboards.

These opportunities require students to try to recreate their memory of the topic. This recreation might not be perfect first time. Repeated practice is required to get it right. Over time, students are able to automatically recall basic knowledge accurately. More complexity can then be added.

Daniel Schacter

WE RECREATE OR RECONSTRUCT OUR EXPERIENCES RATHER THAN RETRIEVE COPIES OF THEM.

Providing plenty of concrete examples helps students to understand abstract concepts and relate them to a real context

As a business or economics specialist, you're a subject expert. But even by simply being an adult, you've gained a wealth of experience. Young students, however, often find it considerably more difficult to apply their answers to a specific context than you, as an expert and adult, might expect.

Daniel Willingham

THE MIND SEEMS TO PREFER THE CONCRETE.

Develop understanding and application skills by presenting lots of examples. This is especially important for unfamiliar concepts, such as contestability or elasticity. Many examples, and non-examples, provide clarity. They model how theory relates to reality. Provide a range of diverse case studies from local, national and global contexts. Select contexts that challenge stereotypes, promote diversity and pique curiosity.

CHAPTER
SUBJECT KNOWLEDGE

08 KNOWING YOUR SUBJECT | 09 ENGLISH | 10 MATHS | 11 SCIENCE | 12 GEOGRAPHY | 13 HISTORY |
14 RELIGIOUS EDUCATION | 15 ART | 16 MUSIC | 17 PHYSICAL EDUCATION | 18 DESIGN & TECHNOLOGY |
19 COMPUTER SCIENCE | **20 BUSINESS & ECONOMICS** | 21 DRAMA | 22 DANCE |

Developing analysis involves showing students how and why things happen so they can explain for themselves

Use Brain Chain Explain to develop high-quality analytical thinking and writing.

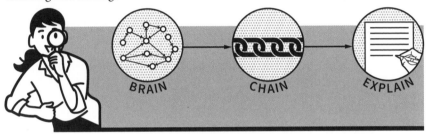

BRAIN   CHAIN   EXPLAIN

Brain

Share your expert 'schema' with students to show them how you think. Use a graphic organiser to do this, such as a flow chart, input-output diagram or concept map. In business, this could include mapping concepts related to 'product' in marketing such as packaging, brand and design, which all contribute to differentiation. Develop a rich and connected visual representation of the topic and encourage students to learn this.

Chain

Encourage students to see questions as having chain 'starts' and 'ends'. In 'Explain the ways a business might differentiate their products', the chain start is 'a way' and the chain end is 'differentiation'. Draw a line with boxes at each end for start and end words – the chain plan. Encourage students to identify logical steps to connect the start and the end along the line.

Explain

Once students understand the chain plan they can write out their explanation in full sentences as a paragraph.

David Didau

🔲

*A SCHEMA… CAN BE THOUGHT OF AS AN INTERCONNECTED WEB OF KNOWLEDGE.
(DIDAU, 2018b)*

➕

ECONOMICS USES COULD INCLUDE:

MONETARY TRANSMISSION MECHANISM

ADJUSTMENT FROM SHORT RUN TO LONG RUN IN PERFECT COMPETITION

EFFECTS OF FISCAL DEFICITS

DRAMA

Let's stop perpetuating the idea that drama is a mostly practical subject – it's not.

Kirsten Johnson
Head of music and drama

'We don't do theory work – we're a practical subject'

As a new teacher it can be very tempting to say that 'drama is a practical subject' when justifying the absence of written work or visible marking, but while there are numerous conversations to be had about exercise books in schools, this is not one of them, as it simply isn't true. Drama is not a practical subject. It is a subject that requires both *knowledge of* and *skill in* the dramatic arts.

Drama lessons can be difficult to manage – so keep to your routines

It is no secret that the absence of desks and the invitation to take their shoes off at the door can lead even the nicest of Year 7 classes a little awry when they enter the drama studio. Help alleviate this sort of disruption by ensuring your classroom routines are clear and enforced from day one – collecting clipboards on the way in for any written work, having a clear seating plan and following school policies for silent starter exercises and so on will create the same classroom environment as the English classroom.

Ensure students know what they are doing

I don't just mean that students should be aware of the classroom routines – students need to know what to do, when to do it, why they are doing it and how to physically do it before they can start acting. Don't be tempted to send the students off to 'make a freeze frame of [insert any theme here]' as they won't know what to do, why they are doing it or even how to do it.

Daniel Willingham

Factual knowledge must precede skill.

1 ▸ 2 ▸ 3 ▸ 4 ▸ 5 ▸ 6

CHAPTER
SUBJECT KNOWLEDGE

08 KNOWING YOUR SUBJECT | 09 ENGLISH | 10 MATHS | 11 SCIENCE | 12 GEOGRAPHY | 13 HISTORY |
14 RELIGIOUS EDUCATION | 15 ART | 16 MUSIC | 17 PHYSICAL EDUCATION | 18 DESIGN & TECHNOLOGY |
19 COMPUTER SCIENCE | 20 BUSINESS & ECONOMICS | **21 DRAMA** | 22 DANCE |

Knowledge begets skill

Introduce theory work from day one in the drama studio – share your enthusiasm for all things dramatic including the *how* and *why*. In order to do, your students must first know.

Scaffold and model everything you want to see

Enable students to be successful in their performance work by modelling what this skill will look like when presented correctly. Break it down into small steps so that students can grasp the intricacies of it – no detail is too ridiculous to include. If you have ever asked a group of students to show you their 'scared' face then you will know that you are usually faced with at least 10 variations. Be specific about what you want to see or you probably won't see it.

Explain the impact of their actions

Students need to understand the impact of their dramatic actions on the audience. That is, after all, the impetus behind acting – being able to exert some form of influence over the emotions of another person. Describe how their acting made you feel, what it made you think of. Encourage students to build their emotional vocabulary in order for them to accurately describe their dramatic intentions.

Above all else, remember that drama is a knowledge-driven subject, not just a practical subject.

DANCE

As a form of expression, dance is limitless and liberating. Dance is accessible for all and can break down many social, physical and language barriers.

Nicky Blackford
Assistant headteacher and dance specialist

Build early success – ignite their passion!

As a dance teacher, you have the ability to motivate and inspire. Use your training to show them the beauty and diversity of movement; from the warm-up to the final performance. It's important to do this in small *steps*. Many KS3 students will not have the prior knowledge to tether this rhythmic movement to, so it's important to rehearse and repeat – allow them to find success from the start. Let the Gradual Release Model (GRM) guide your practice: I do, We do, You do. Show them excellence through modelling, explore through collaborative and creative practice, and motivate them to perform with confidence.

Ron Berger

IF YOU'RE GOING TO DO SOMETHING, I BELIEVE YOU SHOULD DO IT WELL. YOU SHOULD SWEAT OVER IT AND MAKE SURE IT'S STRONG AND ACCURATE AND BEAUTIFUL AND YOU SHOULD BE PROUD OF IT.

Dance can be the optimal blend of direct instruction and 'mode b' teaching (Teaching WalkThrus, Sherrington & Caviglioli)

Freedom to explore in a dance lesson is crucial, and student-led learning for the purposes of creativity and experimentation should be actively encouraged. As with any 'we do' practice though, this collaboration should be guided by the teacher. Before exploring their own ideas, students should have had the appropriate or indeed expert instruction/input/explanation from the teacher to ensure that they are prepared to meet the challenges of the learning tasks. Feedback is a constant feature of any dance classroom and this guidance, as students are discovering, is paramount to their knowledge and skills development.

Speak like a dancer

The importance of oracy is well researched and we cannot shy away from teaching students the language of our subjects, no matter the difficulty. Dance terminology is wondrous in its French (and Russian) roots – empowering students to apply this knowledge and to speak confidently only sets to ignite their passion further!

CHAPTER
SUBJECT KNOWLEDGE

08 KNOWING YOUR SUBJECT | 09 ENGLISH | 10 MATHS | 11 SCIENCE | 12 GEOGRAPHY | 13 HISTORY |
14 RELIGIOUS EDUCATION | 15 ART | 16 MUSIC | 17 PHYSICAL EDUCATION | 18 DESIGN & TECHNOLOGY |
19 COMPUTER SCIENCE | 20 BUSINESS & ECONOMICS | 21 DRAMA | **22 DANCE** |

Whatever the context of your dance lesson, be it mastering the basics of actions, space, dynamics and relationships or the intricacies of a performance's historical context, dance instruction follows the same cycle as any effective lesson: model, practice and feedback. Build their repertoire and watch their creativity thrive!

Model everything

Like any teacher, you are the most powerful resource in the room; never more so than in a practical lesson. The art of demonstration and modelling excellence is key.

Break down the steps

Repetition and deliberate practice is the cornerstone of any dance lesson. Not only for its scaffolding purposes but to build early success. Dance can be daunting for many students so let them feel that sense of achievement early on.

Be faithful to the language

Tier 3 vocabulary in dance is complex. Like MFL and music, it requires not only the mastery of specialist terminology but the idiosyncrasies of a foreign language – *jeté*, *pas de chat*. Embrace it and start as you mean to go on!

PEDAGOGICAL PRINCIPLES

23

COGNITIVE LOAD THEORY
Dylan Wiliam describes John Sweller's cognitive load theory (CLT) as the single most important thing for teachers to know.

24

MANAGING COGNITIVE LOAD
CLT reveals how teachers can help reduce the impacts of cognitive overload.

25

POWERFUL QUESTIONING
Effective questioning will unlock what your students are thinking, helping you check their understanding.

26

EXPLAINING
Carefully crafted explanations introduce new information clearly, cause students to think hard and connect new content to prior knowledge.

31

METACOGNITION
Create opportunities for students to think about their learning.

32

REVISION HABITS PT1
Instilling scholarly habits with your students is all part of the learning process.

33

REVISION HABITS PT2
Vary students' revision diet with independent study strategies.

03

SPREAD

23

COGNITIVE LOAD THEORY

Dylan Wiliam describes John Sweller's cognitive load theory (CLT) as the single most important thing for teachers to know.

John Sweller

Without an understanding of human cognitive architecture, instruction is blind.

Dylan Wiliam

I'VE COME TO THE CONCLUSION SWELLER'S COGNITIVE LOAD THEORY IS THE SINGLE MOST IMPORTANT THING FOR TEACHERS TO KNOW. (WILIAM, 2017)

WORKING MEMORY IS THE CONSCIOUS AND LIMITED COMPONENT OF OUR MEMORY. IT PROCESSES INCOMING AND RETRIEVED INFORMATION.

LONG-TERM MEMORY IS VAST AND STORES INFORMATION THAT HAS BEEN SUCCESSFULLY PROCESSED BY OUR WORKING MEMORY.

Knowledge categories

Cognitive load theory explains how learning happens through a relationship between working memory and long-term memory. David Geary is an evolutionary psychologist whose categories of knowledge provide a framework to help understand this relationship. Geary distinguishes between what he terms biologically primary and biologically secondary knowledge.

Biologically primary knowledge

Biologically primary knowledge is information humans evolved to acquire. It is learned but cannot (easily) be taught. Humans have acquired this knowledge unconsciously as it is essential for survival. This knowledge includes social skills such as speaking, listening and face recognition. Most humans acquire this knowledge with minimal effort.

Biologically secondary knowledge

Biologically secondary knowledge, also known as cultural knowledge, is what our culture deems important. Humans acquire this knowledge in a formal setting – schools, colleges and universities. It is the knowledge teachers need to explicitly teach and not leave for students to discover by themselves. Acquiring this knowledge requires attention and a lot of effort.

Human cognitive architecture

The diagram on the right is a model created by Oliver Caviglioli; it merges CLT with the work of Dan Willingham. It helps simplify the learning process and the relationship between two memory components – working memory and long-term memory.

1 ▸ 2 ▸ **3** ▸ 4 ▸ 5 ▸ 6

CHAPTER
PEDAGOGICAL PRINCIPLES

23 COGNITIVE LOAD THEORY | 24 MANAGING COGNITIVE LOAD | 25 POWERFUL QUESTIONING |
26 EXPLAINING | 27 MODELLING | 28 KNOWLEDGE RETRIEVAL | 29 INCLUSIVE PRACTICE |
30 WORKING WITH TEACHING ASSISTANTS | 31 METACOGNITION | 32 REVISION HABITS PT1 | 33 REVISION PT2 |

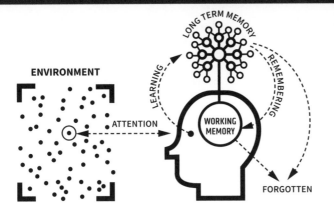

← DIAGRAM USED WITH
PERMISSION FROM
OLIVER CAVIGLIOLI

Daniel Willingham

Working memory is finite

Working memory is the conscious component of memory
where information is temporarily held and manipulated
for learning. Its capacity is limited to seven plus or minus
two items of information at any one time. Humans can
only keep information in their working memory for a short
time. When information is vast, too complex or abstract,
students' working memory will overload.

*UNDERSTANDING IS
REMEMBERING IN
DISGUISE.*

*MEMORY IS THE RESIDUE
OF THOUGHT.*

Long-term memory is infinite

For learning to happen, students must process information
in their working memory and transfer it for storage in
their long-term memory. Information is organised and
structured in the long-term memory into cognitive
frameworks called schema. These schemas activate when
students encounter familiar information. Unlike working
memory, long-term memory is vast. When information
in students' long-term memory is activated, it transfers
back to their working memory. But it does so without any
implications on working memory capacity. Therefore, when
teaching novel information, you should try to activate
similar prior knowledge. To strengthen the connections
between working memory and long-term memory, students
must think hard about the content and encounter key ideas
at least three times.

➕
SCHEMAS ORGANISE,
CATEGORISE AND LINK
CONCEPTS. THEY ARE
THE KNOWLEDGE
STRUCTURES HELD IN
LONG-TERM MEMORY.

SPREAD

24

MANAGING COGNITIVE LOAD

CLT reveals how teachers can help reduce the impacts of cognitive overload.

TRANSIENT INFORMATION

THE SPOKEN WORD IS TRANSIENT. WHEN A TEACHER SPEAKS, STUDENTS CAN BE EASILY OVERWHELMED.

Classroom implications

The transient information effect doesn't mean you need to limit teacher talk. Try to be efficient when talking by chunking instructions and explanations. Use lots of checking for understanding. For example, use Cold Calling and Think, Pair, Share to ensure students have understood your explanations and that the information has not become lost.

INTRINSIC VS EXTRINSIC LOAD

EXTRINSIC LOAD – INFORMATION UNRELATED TO THE LEARNING AT HAND – OVERLOADS STUDENTS' WORKING MEMORY.

Classroom implications

As seen on spread 06, maximise intrinsic load by intentionally developing students' attentional habits. Also, when designing learning resources, remove distracting items. Avoid using fonts that are difficult to read and confusing. Keep resources about the content you wish for them to learn; this applies to printed and electronic resources.

WORKING MEMORY LIMITS

WORKING MEMORY IS FINITE AND EASILY OVERWHELMED WHEN ENCOUNTERING NEW INFORMATION.

Classroom implications

The limitations of working memory can be bypassed by connecting new information to knowledge that already exists in long-term memory. Regular retrieval practice and reviewing of past content can help here. Also, chunk information and frequently check for understanding before introducing the next step. Again, minimise extrinsic load, and maximise intrinsic load.

SPLIT ATTENTION

WHEN LABELS AND ANNOTATIONS FOR A DIAGRAM ARE AT A DISTANCE FROM IT, THIS CAUSES EXTRANEOUS LOAD.

Classroom implications

Avoid having diagrams separated from their relevant labels, explanations and questions. Where possible, place labels as close to their visual counterpart as possible. If a label is likely to obscure elements of the diagram, use arrows.

1 ▸ 2 ▸ 3 ▸ 4 ▸ 5 ▸ 6

CHAPTER
PEDAGOGICAL PRINCIPLES

23 COGNITIVE LOAD THEORY | **24 MANAGING COGNITIVE LOAD** | 25 POWERFUL QUESTIONING |
26 EXPLAINING | 27 MODELLING | 28 KNOWLEDGE RETRIEVAL | 29 INCLUSIVE PRACTICE |
30 WORKING WITH TEACHING ASSISTANTS | 31 METACOGNITION | 32 REVISION HABITS PT1 | 33 REVISION PT2 |

NOVICES AND EXPERTS

STUDENTS ARE NOVICES IN YOUR SUBJECT. THEY THINK DIFFERENTLY ABOUT YOUR DISCIPLINE TO YOU, THE EXPERT.

Classroom implications
As an expert, you have rich interconnected schemas in your long-term memory. Your schemas are organised and allow you to see how the different concepts of your subject connect. Novices need these connections made explicit. Show your students how what they are learning fits within the big picture of your subject.

WORKED EXAMPLES

USING WORKED EXAMPLES MAKES VISIBLE HOW EXPERTS THINK AND SOLVE PROBLEMS.

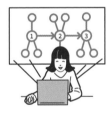

Classroom implications
The goal is for students to become independent learners. But, much like a driving instructor, teachers need to show students what this looks like in practice. Worked examples show students how experts solve problems, breaking the process down into small bite-sized chunks.

GUIDANCE FADING

IF STUDENTS ARE TO BECOME INDEPENDENT, THE TEACHER MUST HAND OVER THE BATON ONCE STUDENTS HAVE A FIRM GRIP.

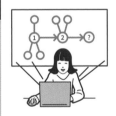

Classroom implications
To build towards independent practice, provide partially completed worked examples. Gradually reduce the scaffolded support when you are confident your students will have independent success. Use the I do, We do, You do strategy on spread 27 to gradually reduce the scaffold you provide your students with.

MODALITY

THE FINITE RESOURCES OF WORKING MEMORY CAN BE EXPANDED BY USING DUAL CODING TO INTRODUCE NEW INFORMATION.

Classroom implications
Our auditory and visual channels absorb information separately, doubling the amount of information we can process. Provide students with a visual to supplement verbal explanations. Doing so has no additional working memory costs but can temporarily boost working memory capacity.

POWERFUL QUESTIONING

Effective questioning will unlock what your students are thinking, helping you check their understanding.

SEE **SPREAD 37 &
SPREAD 38** TO LEARN
MORE ABOUT CHECKING
FOR UNDERSTANDING

Effective questioning

Questions will undoubtedly be one of your most used pedagogy strategies. If we do not ask or answer questions, we cannot be responsive to support and direct learning. The first pillar you will want to develop is how you ask questions and build a culture of open dialogue between you and your students. Always warmly invite students to answer questions. For example, 'Millie, I am really interested to know what you are thinking about...' Doing so will signal to the class you care about what they have to say.

One mistake made by teachers is asking a question, asking students who know the answer to raise their hand, and then calling on one of the students.

**Doug Lemov
(2021)**

Barak Rosenshine

Question, pause, respond

When starting to teach your first class, you will want students to respond to your questions instantaneously. After all, no one wants that period of awkward silence, especially when your mentor is observing you.

*QUESTIONS HELP
STUDENTS PRACTICE
NEW INFORMATION AND
CONNECT NEW MATERIAL
TO THEIR PRIOR LEARNING*

However awkward this might be though, it's important to give students thinking time between asking a question and expecting a response. This gives students a chance to process the question and decide on their response. Model this to students and explain that you will allow them some time to think about their response. On average, teachers will only give students 1.5 seconds to respond. Aim to give students longer. Depending on the complexity of the question, allowing up to one minute will illicit much more thoughtful responses.

'When I ask a question, I don't want you to respond straight away. Take your time to think about how you want to respond.'

CHAPTER
PEDAGOGICAL PRINCIPLES

23 COGNITIVE LOAD THEORY | 24 MANAGING COGNITIVE LOAD | **25 POWERFUL QUESTIONING** |
26 EXPLAINING | 27 MODELLING | 28 KNOWLEDGE RETRIEVAL | 29 INCLUSIVE PRACTICE |
30 WORKING WITH TEACHING ASSISTANTS | 31 METACOGNITION | 32 REVISION HABITS PT1 | 33 REVISION PT2 |

Hidden hurdles

There will be unknown factors that might affect whether students want to answer your questions. For example, peer pressure, fear of failure, or not understanding what the question asked, along with external factors beyond your control. There are several ways you can help to improve your students' willingness to respond to your questions.

SPEND TIME PLANNING OUT WHAT QUESTIONS YOU INTEND TO ASK

Knowing your students

It will be challenging to remember all of your students' names when you first begin teaching. Create a seating plan with photos and have this at hand to help you ask questions.

Establish routines for questioning

Be clear on the expectations for asking and answering questions right from the start. It is important you lay out the expectations and reinforce these in every lesson.

'Remember, when you want to ask a question, you should raise your hand and not shout out.'

'When someone is answering a question, you should track the speaker.'

SEE **SPREAD 03 & SPREAD 04** TO REMIND YOURSELF ABOUT BUILDING RELATIONSHIPS AND ESTABLISHING ROUTINES

Making everyone think

When asking the class a question, you want everyone to be thinking. If you ask a question directly to a student, it tells the rest of the class they do not need to be thinking. Use Doug Lemov's Cold Call and No Opt Out techniques so all students know you might direct the question to them.

EXPLAINING

Carefully crafted explanations introduce new information clearly, cause students to think hard and connect new content to prior knowledge.

The foundations for presenting new information

SEE **SPREAD 08** TO REMIND YOURSELF ABOUT SUBJECT KNOWLEDGE

Behind every great explanation is a great teacher. When you first thought about becoming a teacher, we are sure the idea of talking about something you are passionate about, your subject, will have been a motivating factor. Delivering new and unfamiliar information through your explanations is fundamental for learning.

Evidence Based Education

The challenge is to get your explanations just right by finding a balance.

EFFECTIVE EXPLANATIONS HELP STUDENTS TO DEVELOP FLUENT AND FLEXIBLE NETWORKS OF KNOWLEDGE.

Too easy – – – – – – – – – – – – – – – – **Too complex**

Too short – – – – – – – – – – – – – – – **Too long**

In the Great Teaching Toolkit Evidence Review report, the role of explanation in the classroom is summarised into three core goals:

1. to prepare your students to learn something new;

2. to present new content and ideas to your students; and

3. to connect new ideas to prior knowledge.

Activate prior knowledge

SEE **SPREAD 23** TO REMIND YOURSELF ABOUT COGNITIVE LOAD THEORY.

Accounting for students' prior knowledge will help make your explanations more effective and efficient. Remember, activating prior knowledge can help students acquire new knowledge with less working memory cost. Doing so will build students' schemas as you intentionally reveal links and connections from the get-go. Also, knowing what your students know can help you pitch your explanations at the right level. Vygotsky referred to this as the Zone of Proximal Development.

AN ADAPTED VERSION OF LEV VYGOTSKY'S ZONE OF PROXIMAL DEVELOPMENT.

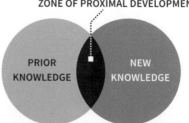

ZONE OF PROXIMAL DEVELOPMENT

PRIOR KNOWLEDGE

NEW KNOWLEDGE

1 → 2 → **3** → 4 → 5 → 6

CHAPTER
PEDAGOGICAL PRINCIPLES

23 COGNITIVE LOAD THEORY | 24 MANAGING COGNITIVE LOAD | 25 POWERFUL QUESTIONING |
26 EXPLAINING | 27 MODELLING | 28 KNOWLEDGE RETRIEVAL | 29 INCLUSIVE PRACTICE |
30 WORKING WITH TEACHING ASSISTANTS | 31 METACOGNITION | 32 REVISION HABITS PT 1 | 33 REVISION PT 2 |

The art of presenting new information

Consider how you will present new information to your students. Daniel Willingham suggests creating memorable moments through the power of stories. Our cognitive architecture is tuned to understand and remember stories because they are more interesting. When presenting new content, share stories from your own experiences.

Take time to prepare how you will deliver your explanations and rehearse them. Cut out any unnecessary elements that may act as distractors and overload working memory. Remember your audience. When learning something new, the predominant situation in a classroom, students need content broken down. Identify the technical vocabulary you will use and consider pre-teaching it. Supplement your explanations with lots of checking for understanding to check students are grasping the content. All of these tips will help make your explanations more memorable.

Alex Quigley

GREAT EXPLANATIONS, LIKE ALL ASPECTS OF TEACHING, CAN BE REPEATEDLY HONED AND IMPROVED.
(QUIGLEY, 2013)

Modelling and worked examples

Using worked examples can help reduce the burden on working memory, giving students space to process new information by providing them with a step-by-step guide to tackling a task. Research indicates that when students are learning something new, providing two to three worked examples can help the learning process. Bob Pritchard (EEF) suggests using the FAME approach to implementing worked examples in your classroom.

SEE **SPREAD 27** TO READ HOW MODELLING CAN REINFORCE YOUR EXPLANATIONS.

FADING – The process of gradually reducing and removing worked examples.

ALTERNATING – Vary your use of worked examples across the lesson.

MISTAKES – As students' knowledge grows, provide examples containing mistakes.

EXPLANATION – Model your thought process as you present a worked example.

MODELLING

Modelling is a form of scaffolding that makes it more likely students can access work above their pay grade.

Fully Guided |
teacher led

1 I do — Fully
worked examples

2 We do — Partially
worked examples
& guided practice

No guidance |
students are
independent

3 You do —
Independent
practice

Modelling is a type of scaffolding. Like all scaffolds, eventually, this support must come down. This diagram captures the movement from highly scaffolded instruction to independent work.

Jo Morgan

*A KEY PART OF ANY
TEACHER'S JOB IS
MODELLING.*

*LIVE MODELLING UNDER
A VISUALISER IS SUCH A
HELPFUL TECHNIQUE,
PARTICULARLY WHEN
YOU ARE TEACHING
SOMETHING PRACTICAL.*

Modelling helps manage cognitive load

Effective modelling lets students peek behind the curtain – it makes the implicit explicit. Modelling helps manage cognitive load as students aren't juggling the procedures of a task and their application simultaneously. Also, the teacher doesn't leave students to 'figure it out' for themselves. As novices, students are easily overwhelmed, and such methods will not develop confidence. A driving instructor would be sacked for negligence if they allowed clients to 'figure it out'. Effective teachers show students how to do things and check they have understood before engineering opportunities for independent practice.

Live modelling

There are different modelling approaches a teacher can use. You might create your models in advance in PowerPoint, Keynote or Slides. Alternatively, and our preferred method, you model live. Modelling live will require you to use a visualiser or an interactive whiteboard. You save time as you are not creating presentations containing intricate animations. Instead, use the time to design meaningful practice tasks and prepare powerful questions.

Live modelling is valuable in all phases and subjects. If you are nervous, don't be. As your subject and pedagogical knowledge grow, so too will your confidence. Counter your nerves by scripting your models and explanations.

1 → 2 → 3 → 4 → 5 → 6

CHAPTER
PEDAGOGICAL PRINCIPLES

23 COGNITIVE LOAD THEORY | 24 MANAGING COGNITIVE LOAD | 25 POWERFUL QUESTIONING |
26 EXPLAINING | **27 MODELLING** | 28 KNOWLEDGE RETRIEVAL | 29 INCLUSIVE PRACTICE |
30 WORKING WITH TEACHING ASSISTANTS | 31 METACOGNITION | 32 REVISION HABITS PT1 | 33 REVISION PT2 |

I do, We do, You do

I do, We do, You do makes explicit the underlying thinking of learning processes. It's a carefully scaffolded approach, moving from highly structured teacher instruction and guided practice to students working independently. The key to getting this technique right is to master the 'We do' phase.

I do

Fully model how to complete a task or problem. Model it live, narrating your thinking as you write. Check students' understanding by asking questions about each step of the model answer. Provide a second fully worked example. Highlight the ways the new model is similar and different to the previous. Doing so will reinforce the main ideas of the solution/method.

We do

The 'We do' phase is key to successful modelling. Design guided practice tasks that obtain high rates of student success. Students should get a sense of how success feels while working towards independent practice. Gradually reduce the level of support to build towards independence. If students struggle, provide more guided practice.

You do

Independent learning should only happen when there is *enough knowledge in the room*. Use checks for understanding to ensure a high success rate – students answer approximately 80% of the questions correctly. In a mixed-ability class, 80% might be more realistic over a series of lessons. During independent practice, students should recall knowledge from memory.

As students transition from the 'We do' and 'You do' phases, there is a vital interchange between modelling, checking for understanding and feedback. Checking for understanding will tell you how many students have grasped the procedures in your model. And feedback will help nudge along those students that haven't.

IT IS UNLIKELY YOU WILL USE ALL THREE STEPS EVERY LESSON. MOST LESSONS WILL INCLUDE THE 'I DO' AND 'WE DO' PHASES, BUT INDEPENDENT PRACTICE SHOULD ONLY HAPPEN WHEN STUDENTS HAVE KNOWLEDGE FOR SUCCESS.

Paul Kirschner & Carl Hendrick

YOU CAN'T COMMUNICATE ABOUT SOMETHING, WRITE ABOUT SOMETHING, DISCUSS OR ARGUE ABOUT SOMETHING ETC. WITHOUT FIRST KNOWING ABOUT THAT SOMETHING AND THEN ALSO KNOWING THE RULES (I.E. THE PROCEDURES) FOR DOING IT.

Tom Sherrington

WHAT IS NEEDED IS A MUCH MORE EXTENDED HAND-OVER WHERE THE TEACHER WORKS WITH THE STUDENTS TO DO THE TASK TOGETHER. (SHERRINGTON, 2020)

SPREAD

28

KNOWLEDGE RETRIEVAL

Recalling taught knowledge is key to strengthening the connection between working and long-term memory.

What is retrieval practice?

SEE **SPREAD 23** TO REFER BACK TO COGNITIVE LOAD THEORY.

Retrieval practice is a strategy you can use to get students to think hard and bring information back to their working memory. To increase students' fluency and accuracy when retrieving knowledge, you need to provide plenty of opportunities for students to recall and use what they have previously learned. Doing so helps strengthen the connection between working memory and long-term memory. Just like a musician will spend hours practising playing an instrument, students need to do the same with the knowledge they acquire so they don't lose it.

Kate Jones

BY USING RETRIEVAL PRACTICE, STUDENTS RECALL PREVIOUSLY LEARNT KNOWLEDGE WHICH CREATES STRONGER MEMORY TRACES.

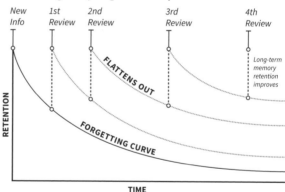

The forgetting curve

WHEN PLANNING YOUR LESSONS CONSIDER THE MOST IMPORTANT INFORMATION THAT YOU WANT STUDENTS TO REMEMBER.

The Ebbinghaus forgetting curve illustrates what can happen when we don't recall information. His study shows that our ability to retrieve learned knowledge diminishes over time. However, when we introduce regular spaced reviews, this helps to improve long-term retention.

Tips for meaningful retrieval practice

TIP 1: When using retrieval practice, keep it low stakes to reduce anxiety. Let your students know there won't be any grades associated with this knowledge recall.

TIP 2: Explain to your students why retrieval practice can help with their long-term retention of knowledge.

```
1 → 2 → 3 → 4 → 5 → 6
```

CHAPTER
PEDAGOGICAL PRINCIPLES

23 COGNITIVE LOAD THEORY | 24 MANAGING COGNITIVE LOAD | 25 POWERFUL QUESTIONING |
26 EXPLAINING | 27 MODELLING | **28 KNOWLEDGE RETRIEVAL** | 29 INCLUSIVE PRACTICE |
30 WORKING WITH TEACHING ASSISTANTS | 31 METACOGNITION | 32 REVISION HABITS PT1 | 33 REVISION PT2 |

TIP 3: Ensure students recall knowledge from memory without the help of their class notes so that they don't simply copy information.

TIP 4: To increase their chances of building vast and meaningful schemas, direct students to retrieve knowledge with links to the new content they will learn in the current lesson. Follow this up by making these links explicit.

TIP 5: Emerging evidence from neuroscience indicates priming improves retrieval practice. Priming is when the teacher allows students to rehearse before retrieving. For example, before a quiz, students explain to a peer a concept(s) you intend to quiz them on. After the priming phase, students retrieve knowledge unassisted.

Retrieval in action
There are many strategies you can use to get students to retrieve knowledge. Here are some examples we have found to work.

Brain dump
Without any assistance from their notes, students write everything they can remember about a topic they have been studying. Give students a blank piece of paper and set them a timeframe for the knowledge recall.

Quizzing – distributed questions
Create a series of questions to get students to recall knowledge. Create questions to sample recently taught content (the last few lessons), older content (within weeks of the lesson) and even older content (previous topics). Be strategic with these questions based on prior knowledge gaps and any links to new knowledge you will teach in the lesson.

Flashcards and knowledge organisers
Refer to spreads 32 and 33 on revision habits, where we explain how students can engage in independent and peer retrieval using flashcards and knowledge organisers. Students can engage in peer knowledge retrieval by asking each other questions from flashcards or a knowledge organiser.

Dr Pooja K. Agarwal

RETRIEVAL PRACTICE HELPS STUDENTS 'USE IT OR LOSE IT', JUST LIKE PRACTICING A LANGUAGE OR AN INSTRUMENT.

NEUROSCIENTISTS BELIEVE PRIMING STRENGTHENS THE NEURAL PATHWAYS BETWEEN WORKING MEMORY AND LONG-TERM MEMORY.

WHILE KNOWLEDGE RETRIEVAL TASKS LEND THEMSELVES WELL TO THE START OF THE LESSON, THEY CAN BE DEPLOYED AT ANY TIME.

SPREAD

29

INCLUSIVE PRACTICE
Key considerations for planning lessons that enable all
learners to access and progress.

Katherine Walsh
Trust lead for
inclusion

Demystifying SEND
Special educational needs and disabilities (SEND)
encompasses a vast range of individual needs. As a teacher,
at times it may feel as though you need to be an expert on
every special educational need – this is not the case. Your
role is to plan and teach well-structured lessons and to be
curious about the children and young people you teach,
noticing when they do well and where they struggle. It is
important to remember that with or without an identified
SEND, all learners have strengths and weaknesses that can
impact on their learning in the classroom. As a teacher,
your role is to regularly reflect on your practice and adapt
your teaching where necessary to enable all learners to
engage with and make progress in the curriculum.

Margaret Mulholland

*The inclusive teacher challenges [the] mindset that
seeks to predetermine the capacity of each learner,
replacing it instead with a curiosity about what the
learner can achieve.*

The language we use matters
The acronyms next to a child or young person's name on
a register or seating plan do not define them as a learner,
so it is important that the language we use also does not.
Consider the statement 'he is SEND' – does it help you
teach the learner? Using labels in this way can limit our
thinking on what a learner can achieve and unintentionally
put a ceiling on their potential. Changing 'is' to 'has' – 'he
has SEND' – can reframe your thinking, bringing the
learner to the forefront and not the diagnostic label. Best
practice is to describe your observations of a learner, e.g.
'He struggles to retain new learning from one lesson to the
next.' This information can help you work with colleagues
to determine teaching strategies that can support the child
or young person's learning in the classroom.

CHAPTER
PEDAGOGICAL PRINCIPLES

23 COGNITIVE LOAD THEORY | 24 MANAGING COGNITIVE LOAD | 25 POWERFUL QUESTIONING |
26 EXPLAINING | 27 MODELLING | 28 KNOWLEDGE RETRIEVAL | **29 INCLUSIVE PRACTICE** |
30 WORKING WITH TEACHING ASSISTANTS | 31 METACOGNITION | 32 REVISION HABITS PT1 | 33 REVISION PT2 |

High-quality teaching strategies will support all learners, including learners with SEND

Avoid planning lessons for all children, and then thinking about children and young people with SEND. Plan lessons with inclusive teaching strategies as a part of your standard classroom practice. Spreads in this book that are highly relevant for learners with SEND are: 'Establishing Routines', 'Explanations' and 'Modelling'.

Having inclusive teaching strategies as standard classroom practice enables you to 'zoom in' on learners who are not making expected progress. Remember to focus on what a learner can do – this is just as important as identifying the things they find challenging. Are there parts of the lesson when they are more engaged, e.g. the start of the lesson or during class discussions? Are there certain topics they engage in more than others? This information can help you begin to identify potential barriers to learning.

You are not alone

The diverse nature of SEND can sometimes make teaching feel overwhelming. There will be times when you will find it a challenge to teach one of your classes. There will also be times when you struggle to identify what is happening for a learner – academically, socially or emotionally. When you feel this way, it can be helpful to:

Reflect on your practice. How clear are your routines? Are the social dynamics of the classroom managed effectively enough?

Draw on the knowledge of your colleagues, e.g. teachers who have previously taught the class/learner or currently teach a different subject.

Talk to the learner(s). Are there strategies or scaffolds that could support their learning?

This information can help you identify teaching strategies to support learners in your lesson, as well as begin to recognise individual barriers to learning.

WORKING WITH TEACHING ASSISTANTS

When teachers work closely with their TAs, students' chances of flourishing increase.

What the research says

Teaching assistants are an essential resource at a school's disposal. The EEF guidance report on 'Making Best Use of Teaching Assistants' found that teachers value TAs as motivators and confidence builders. But the report also reviews overwhelming evidence that points to schools not effectively deploying their TAs.

The main concern the report expresses is TAs can unknowingly encourage dependency. One-to-one support can negatively affect students' ownership of their learning. There is also a worry TAs prioritise task completion over student learning, meaning students can get away without thinking or acting for themselves. But the blame should not reside with TAs because: 'Simply put, research suggests it is the decisions made about TAs by school leaders and teachers, not decisions made by TAs, that best explain the effects of TA support in the classroom on student progress. In other words, don't blame TAs!'

How to effectively deploy TAs

TAs are at their best when they have had the time to meet with teachers before and after lessons. TAs are far more likely to feel valued when given the opportunity to work collaboratively. Find the time to meet with them, ensuring they know their role in your classroom. Use the opportunity to discuss and share 'schemes of work' and resources, ensuring they have the relevant subject knowledge to support you. Don't forget to explain how the content students learn fits within a careful sequence. And provide them with exemplar work.

The illustration on the right-hand side is based on the EEF guidance report's recommendations. Use it to frame your conversation with TAs so that students don't become overly dependent on TA support. You'll get more bang for your buck by asking your TA to monitor students' attentional habits during your explanations and when you are modelling. Also, deploy them as an extra pair of eyes and ears during checking for understanding.

CHAPTER
PEDAGOGICAL PRINCIPLES

23 COGNITIVE LOAD THEORY | 24 MANAGING COGNITIVE LOAD | 25 POWERFUL QUESTIONING |
26 EXPLAINING | 27 MODELLING | 28 KNOWLEDGE RETRIEVAL | 29 INCLUSIVE PRACTICE |
30 WORKING WITH TEACHING ASSISTANTS | 31 METACOGNITION | 32 REVISION HABITS PT1 | 33 REVISION PT2 |

Self-scaffolding
The TA's standard position should be to observe, giving students time to think and work independently. Students should retain responsibility for their learning.

Prompting
Prompting is the first line of intervention, only implemented when a student has tried working through the problem independently. A prompt is a gentle nudge like asking, 'What's your first step?'

Clueing
The TA might give a clue when a student has tried working independently and when a prompt has not helped. A clue is a question or a small snippet of information to get the student going.

Modelling
Sometimes students benefit from more modelling and worked examples. A competent TA can model and direct a student to replicate their steps. Again, TAs should try steps 1-3 first.

Correcting
Correcting should be avoided as much as possible. It requires zero independence as the TA corrects a student's work or provides them with an answer.

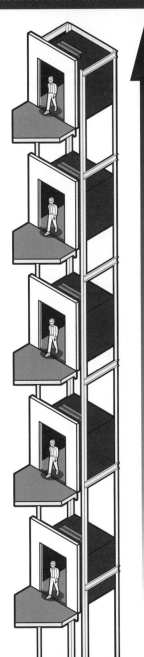

GREATER STUDENT INDEPENDENCE

METACOGNITION

Create opportunities for students to think about their learning.

What the research says

Metacognition is how students monitor and self-regulate their learning. It involves students selecting a strategy to tackle a problem or task. During the process, students must monitor the technique's effectiveness and adjust (or not) accordingly.

The first step to metacognition is getting students to think about their own learning, providing the foundations to support students to plan, monitor, and evaluate their learning. Jennifer Webb divides metacognition into three strands:

Jennifer Webb

⏹

A TEACHER WHO USES METACOGNITIVE APPROACHES AS A FRAMEWORK FOR THEIR TEACHING IS ABLE TO TRAIN THEIR STUDENTS, OVER TIME ...

Metacognitive knowledge is the extent to which a student has knowledge about the task they are completing, knowledge about themselves, and an awareness of what strategies will help them complete the task set.

Metacognitive regulation is the extent to which a student can plan, monitor and evaluate their own learning while completing the task.

Metacognitive motivation is the extent to which a student wants to perform a task. It is also about their interest in the task and how confident they feel about the likelihood they will succeed.

There is a difference between students doing metacognition and behaving metacognitively. For students to behave metacognitively, it takes time and requires a high degree of competence around the three strands outlined above. For example, when students undertake a task, such as answering a question in geography, they should plan a strategy for how to answer the question, monitor their performance while writing their answer, and then evaluate their success.

CHAPTER
PEDAGOGICAL PRINCIPLES

23 COGNITIVE LOAD THEORY | 24 MANAGING COGNITIVE LOAD | 25 POWERFUL QUESTIONING |
26 EXPLAINING | 27 MODELLING | 28 KNOWLEDGE RETRIEVAL | 29 INCLUSIVE PRACTICE |
30 WORKING WITH TEACHING ASSISTANTS | **31 METACOGNITION** | 32 REVISION HABITS PT1 | 33 REVISION PT2 |

The EEF's seven-step model for metacognition

The EEF outline a seven-step model to show how teachers should shift the responsibility from themselves to the students – all scaffolds must come down and make way for independent practice.

THE DIAGRAM BELOW IS ADOPTED FROM THE EEF'S METACOGNITION AND SELF-REGULATED LEARNING GUIDANCE REPORT. (EEF, 2018b)

STAGE	STUDENT / TEACHER	EXAMPLE
1 ACTIVATING PRIOR KNOWLEDGE		*A DAILY REVIEW TO ACTIVATE PRIOR KNOWLEDGE*
2 EXPLICIT STRATEGY INSTRUCTION		*DEMONSTRATING TO STUDENTS HOW TO COMPLETE STEP-BY-STEP BEFORE THEY BEGIN*
3 MODELLING OF LEARNED STRATEGY		*MODEL THE THOUGHT PROCESS TO STUDENTS – 'I WOULD APPROACH IT…'*
4 MEMORISATION OF THE STRATEGY		*'WITH THE PERSON NEXT TO YOU REFLECT ON MY APPROACH.'*
5 GUIDED PRACTICE		*'LET'S GO THROUGH THIS EXAMPLE TOGETHER.'*
6 INDEPENDENT PRACTICE		*'I NOW WANT YOU TO WRITE YOUR OWN ANSWER.'*
7 STRUCTURED REFLECTION		*'WITH THE PERSON NEXT TO YOU, REFLECT ON WHETHER YOU HAVE MET THE SUCCESS CRITERIA.'*

81

REVISION HABITS PT1

Instilling scholarly habits with your students is all part of the learning process.

⬀ REFER BACK TO **SPREAD 28** TO READ ABOUT KNOWLEDGE RETRIEVAL.

Why it is important to develop revision habits with your students

Without guidance, most students will leave revising for their formal internal and external assessments until a few weeks before their exam. As you have learned from the previous spread on knowledge retrieval, leaving all their revision until a few weeks beforehand is counterproductive and will likely lead to underperformance. Therefore, your role as the teacher is to promote effective study habits right from the beginning of the academic year, providing plenty of opportunities for your students to practise effective revision strategies both inside and outside the classroom.

John Dunlosky

💬

STUDENTS BELIEVE THESE RELATIVELY INEFFECTIVE STRATEGIES ARE ACTUALLY THE MOST EFFECTIVE.

In 'Strengthening the Student Toolbox', John Dunlosky highlights that many students will believe they are preparing effectively for their exams through strategies that might include highlighting their notes and rereading information several times before copying it down on another piece of paper. Ultimately, these strategies will yield low success in retaining information over a long period. The diagram below shows the effectiveness of common study techniques.

LEAST EFFECTIVE   **MOST EFFECTIVE**

➕

WHATEVER TECHNIQUES YOU USE WITH YOUR STUDENTS, YOU NEED TO EXPLICITLY INSTRUCT AND MODEL THEIR APPLICATION FOR THEM TO BE EFFECTIVE.

LOW UTILITY	MODERATE UTILITY	HIGH UTILITY
SUMMARISATION	ELABORATIVE INTERROGATION	PRACTICE TESTING
HIGHLIGHTING	SELF-EXPLANATION	DISTRIBUTED (SPACED) PRACTICE
KEYWORD MNEMONIC	INTERLEAVED PRACTICE	
IMAGERY USE FOR TEXT LEARNING		
REREADING		

CHAPTER
PEDAGOGICAL PRINCIPLES

23 COGNITIVE LOAD THEORY | 24 MANAGING COGNITIVE LOAD | 25 POWERFUL QUESTIONING |
26 EXPLAINING | 27 MODELLING | 28 KNOWLEDGE RETRIEVAL | 29 INCLUSIVE PRACTICE |
30 WORKING WITH TEACHING ASSISTANTS | 31 METACOGNITION | **32 REVISION HABITS PT1** | 33 REVISION PT2 |

Using flashcards to distribute practice

One effective learning technique indicated by Dunlosky to
support longer-term retention of knowledge is distributed
(spaced) practice, which students can do through the use
of flashcards. Flashcards have a question, statement or list
of prompts on one side and the answer(s) on their reverse.
For flashcards to be effective, the knowledge needs to be
quizzable. Therefore, it is important to model to students
how to create an effective flashcard, reinforcing that there
shouldn't be too much information on each one.

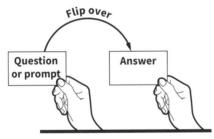

Set aside time at the beginning or end of lessons or homework for students to create their flashcards. Once students
have mastered the art of creating effective flashcards, you
need to model how to use them by demonstrating the
Leitner System, shown below.

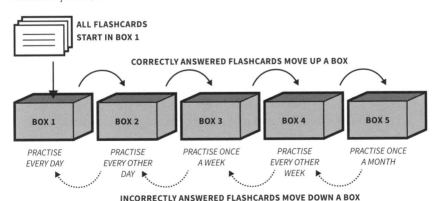

SPREAD

33

REVISION HABITS PT2
Vary students' revision diet with independent study strategies.

Activate students as a learning resource for themselves and one another

You can train students to self-quiz and support each other in building confidence and fluency. Using a knowledge organiser or equivalent resource, students can quiz themselves and each other. Make sure the resource contains quizzable knowledge and invest time to train students on how to use it.

If students are to successfully use one another as a learning resource, you will need to show them how and have structured routines. These routines will likely include giving a specific timeframe, signalling when students should changeover, and how you will monitor the room and check for understanding.

If you want your students to provide expansive answers, then model how to use elaborative questions. The use of elaborative questions involves students answering 'How?', 'Why?' and 'What?' These sorts of questions explore processes, cause and effect, and making predictions.

To get the most out of elaborative questioning, give the students asking questions a resource, such as question stems. You should check for accuracy by monitoring the questioning process. Ensure that whenever necessary, students in their pairs are providing corrective feedback by referring to their resources.

Folding Frenzy

Folding Frenzy is an innovative revision technique created by Simon Beale. It combines different revision techniques in a structured manner and requires students to retrieve knowledge in multiple ways. Also, the finished resource is useful for peer and self-quizzing.

1 → 2 → **3** → 4 → 5 → 6

CHAPTER
PEDAGOGICAL PRINCIPLES

23 COGNITIVE LOAD THEORY | 24 MANAGING COGNITIVE LOAD | 25 POWERFUL QUESTIONING |
26 EXPLAINING | 27 MODELLING | 28 KNOWLEDGE RETRIEVAL | 29 INCLUSIVE PRACTICE |
30 WORKING WITH TEACHING ASSISTANTS | 31 METACOGNITION | 32 REVISION HABITS PT1 | **33 REVISION PT2** |

Simon Beale's Folding Frenzy
—

A Folding Frenzy is a multilayered revision technique that uses a range of strategies in one package to rigorously encode and synthesise knowledge for better retrieval during exams.

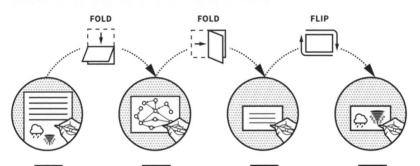

Notes	**Graphic Organiser**	**Flashcard**	**Symbols**
Students write a page of notes on a piece of blank paper on a specifically chosen topic, focusing on key vocabulary, summarising content and symbols/images.	Students then create a graphic organiser representing the core terminology of the notes; mind maps work well.	Students write down 5/6 keywords that summarise the topic.	Students use the symbols from their original notes to illustrate their understanding.

CURRICULUM & ASSESSMENT

34

CURRICULUM KNOWLEDGE
The curriculum is at the heart of what schools do. It is complex and will need a lot of your attention.

35

FORMATIVE ASSESSMENT
Effective learning requires teachers to adapt to the needs of their students and to place students at the heart of the learning process.

36

LEARNING INTENTIONS
Effective learning intentions and success criteria help students understand where they are, where they are going and how to get there.

37

CHECK FOR UNDERSTANDING PT1
Checking for understanding will tell you if it is safe to move on – check students' fluency before teaching new content.

42

READING
At the heart of an ambitious knowledge-rich curriculum is an intentional effort to help students read.

43

DELIBERATE VOCABULARY DEVELOPMENT
Students with broad and rich vocabularies will learn more, remember more and be able to access a rich and demanding curriculum.

44

TEACH TO THE TOP
Students have the right to a demanding and challenging curriculum; a curriculum that does not limit what they can learn and how far they can go.

45

RESOURCE DESIGN
Despite their obvious benefits, most teachers aren't taught how to design resources.

04

CURRICULUM KNOWLEDGE

The curriculum is at the heart of what schools do.
It is complex and will need a lot of your attention.

✚ Why a knowledge-rich curriculum matters

In the words of Sam Strickland, the curriculum is God. The phrase 'knowledge-rich' is now firmly established in teachers' and leaders' lexicon and is synonymous with the curriculum. The shift from 21st-century skills to a knowledge-rich curriculum has been welcome by most professionals in the sector. For two decades, education's quest to find a silver bullet led to teachers and leaders trying to teach transferable skills. Schools constructed curriculums around Bloom's Taxonomy and invested heavily in learning styles and unstructured discovery-based learning. Thankfully, recent developments have paved the way for schools to develop more ambitious and empowering curriculum models.

Knowledge empowers students, helping them to become critical thinkers. After all, what are students meant to analyse and evaluate if they don't have knowledge? Also, in the words of E. D. Hirsch, knowledge begets knowledge. The more students know, the more they can learn. There is also a moral argument for students' entitlement to an ambitious knowledge-rich curriculum. In her book, *Curriculum: Theory, Culture and the Subject Specialisms*, Ruth Ashbee suggests there are four moral arguments for students' right to an ambitious curriculum.

Ruth Ashbee

❞

*KNOWLEDGE IS RICH;
IT EXISTS IN LAYERS OF
MEANING AND IS SO MUCH
MORE THAN A SET OF
SPECIFICATION BULLET
POINTS OR A LIST OF
LESSON TITLES.*

- Cognitive – Cognitive science suggests what students know determines what they can learn. Knowledgeable students can call on their ever-developing schemas to solve problems and improve their thinking.

- Socioeconomic – Access to knowledge increases the likelihood of students gaining excellent qualifications, improving their socioeconomic outlook.

- Democratic – Knowledgeable students will be better able to question and challenge what is happening in society and politics.

- Intellectual – Ashbee argues students have a societal entitlement to knowledge passed down by generations.

CHAPTER
CURRICULUM & ASSESSMENT

34 CURRICULUM KNOWLEDGE | 35 FORMATIVE ASSESSMENT | 36 LEARNING INTENTIONS | 37 CHECK FOR UNDERSTANDING PT1 | 38 CHECK FOR UNDERSTANDING PT2 | 39 GUIDED FEEDBACK | 40 COMPONENTS & COMPOSITES | 41 HOME LEARNING | 42 READING | 43 DELIBERATE VOCABULARY DEVELOPMENT | 44 TEACH TO THE TOP | 45 RESOURCE DESIGN |

Types of knowledge

Knowledge comes in many forms.

TYPES OF KNOWLEDGE

Substantive knowledge	Disciplinary knowledge	Declarative knowledge	Procedural knowledge
includes the ideas, facts and concepts students should know. In geography, this includes features of a river.	includes the traditional processes required to study the subject. In science, students perform experiments to test hypotheses.	includes the key facts students need to know. In history, this includes knowing the Battle of Hastings occurred in 1066.	is what students need to know to perform a task. For example, how to construct an essay in English.

+

THE TYPES OF KNOWLEDGE ARE UNIQUE TO EACH SUBJECT. FOR EXAMPLE, AN ESSAY WRITTEN IN AN ENGLISH LESSON WILL BE DIFFERENT TO AN ESSAY WRITTEN IN SCIENCE, HISTORY OR GEOGRAPHY. THEREFORE, THEY NEED TO BE TAUGHT DIFFERENTLY.

Curriculum considerations

Curriculum planning needs to consider cognitive load theory. Students' limited working memory and prior knowledge are limiting factors when accessing an ambitious curriculum. Mapping out the curriculum coherently and ensuring key concepts are revisited is an effective way to manage students' limited working memory and account for prior knowledge. Teachers need to plan to revisit topics at increasing levels of difficulty, deepening students' understanding while building knowledge on secure foundations. Also, effectively enacting the curriculum requires teachers to be competent at explaining, modelling, checking for understanding and designing practice tasks.

↗

REFER BACK TO **CHAPTER 2** TO LEARN MORE ABOUT SUBJECT KNOWLEDGE.

Tom Sherrington

IT'S UNCONTROVERSIAL – UNCONTESTED – THAT READING FLUENCY IS A KEY COMPONENT IN STUDENTS' WIDER LEARNING CAPACITY AND CONFIDENCE AND YET IT IS ACTUALLY POSSIBLE FOR SOME STUDENTS TO GO THROUGH A SCHOOL DAY OR WEEK WITHOUT DOING VERY MUCH READING AT ALL. (SHERRINGTON, 2022)

Reading fluency is key to students' capacity to learn. Reading should be a regular part of the curriculum diet and not an afterthought when planning the curriculum. As such, we have dedicated spread 42 to reading.

Finally, diversifying the curriculum is crucial in helping students know their place in the world. Bennie Kara says we need to expand beyond our established canon of Western European knowledge. She explains how using role models and stories from outside Western Europe can help create global citizens. Diversifying the curriculum means students receive a more balanced perspective of knowledge.

FORMATIVE ASSESSMENT

Effective learning requires teachers to adapt to the needs of their students and to place students at the heart of the learning process.

Dylan Wiliam

Formative assessment in a nutshell

Dylan Wiliam argues that attending to formative assessment makes more difference to student achievement than anything else we can do. Formative assessment places students at the centre of the learning process. The teacher uses evidence about her students and adapts her teaching. Teachers should prioritise high-quality formative assessment over task completion to ensure learning happens at a deep and meaningful level. To help teachers better implement formative assessment, Siobhán Leahy and Dylan Wiliam chunk various strategies into five strands: *learning intentions | eliciting evidence | feedback | activating students as a learning resource for one another | activating students as owners of their own learning.*

Learning intentions

REFER TO **SPREAD 36** TO LEARN ABOUT LEARNING INTENTIONS.

Sharing learning intentions is common practice in most schools these days. But high-quality formative assessment requires students to understand learning intentions, not just be told them. Students need to understand where they are, where they are going, and what they need to do to get there. When planning learning intentions, you should consider your students' prior knowledge and how the objectives reinforce your curriculum. Plan learning intentions for a sequence of lessons – in some cases, it will be unrealistic for your students to achieve what you set out in one lesson. In spread 36, you will learn more about creating good learning intentions.

Eliciting evidence

REFER TO **SPREAD 25, SPREAD 37 & SPREAD 38** TO LEARN MORE ABOUT QUESTIONING AND CHECKING FOR UNDERSTANDING.

Eliciting evidence involves using a range of activities to assess where students are in relation to the learning intentions. Questioning, discussions and written exercises provide teachers with evidence about how students are doing. Learning activities act as servants to learning intentions and should allow students to communicate their developing understanding.

Teachers must use evidence to adapt their teaching for formative assessment to be purposeful. Also, the evidence

1 → 2 → 3 → 4 → 5 → 6

CHAPTER
CURRICULUM & ASSESSMENT

34 CURRICULUM KNOWLEDGE | **35 FORMATIVE ASSESSMENT** | 36 LEARNING INTENTIONS | 37 CHECK FOR UNDERSTANDING PT1 |
38 CHECK FOR UNDERSTANDING PT2 | 39 GUIDED FEEDBACK | 40 COMPONENTS & COMPOSITES | 41 HOME LEARNING |
42 READING | 43 DELIBERATE VOCABULARY DEVELOPMENT | 44 TEACH TO THE TOP | 45 RESOURCE DESIGN |

should account for all students. Directing the same students to answer questions will likely elicit the correct answers and ensure you get through all of your lesson slides. But it means you and those not answering not knowing where they are in their learning journey. Plus, it implies that most of the class doesn't need to think, and their voice doesn't matter.

Feedback

Feedback should provide clear guidance about how students have performed against the learning intentions. When the success criteria and learning intentions are clear and understood, students can take more ownership of the feedback process. An important part of the feedback process is engineering opportunities for students to apply their feedback to new situations. For example, you might direct students to redraft work or use their knowledge to tackle new but similar problems.

REFER TO **SPREAD 39** TO LEARN ABOUT FEEDBACK.

Activating students as a learning resource for one another

Highly structured collaborative learning can result in learning gains. Group work is most effective when students have existing knowledge about the content they are learning. When this is the case, students can teach others, helping them consolidate their own understanding. Peer assessment, when effectively implemented, helps orient students in relation to learning intentions. Using clear success criteria and exemplar work can boost the effectiveness of peer assessment.

Activating students as owners of their own learning

Self-assessment should help students understand what they have achieved and what else they need to learn in relation to the curriculum. Self-assessment is challenging as it can be emotionally charged. To manage this, have students study samples of others' work. Use work from previous or other groups. Doing so will improve students' understanding of what good work looks like and help them spot errors in their own work.

SPREAD

36

LEARNING INTENTIONS

Effective learning intentions and success criteria help students understand where they are, where they are going and how to get there.

Getting from A to B

Learning intentions should give students the lay of the land for a series of lessons. Effective use of learning intentions 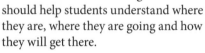 should help students understand where they are, where they are going and how they will get there.

It helps to have the endpoint in mind when creating learning intentions to prioritise the learning and not the activities you will deploy. The learning tasks you design will be important, but act as servants to the learning intentions, helping students acquire the core knowledge you have set out. Purposeful learning activities help students communicate their growing understanding of the knowledge you intend for them to learn.

Tom Sherrington & Oliver Caviglioli

*GOOD LEARNING OBJECTIVES WILL INCLUDE: THE SPECIFIC FACTS, CONCEPTS OR PROCEDURES STUDENTS SHOULD KNOW AND UNDERSTAND, BUILDING ON THE KNOWLEDGE THEY ALREADY HAVE.
(SHERRINGTON & CAVIGLIOLI, 2021)*

If learning intentions tell students where they are going, success criteria help teachers and students monitor how the journey is going. Effective success criteria make explicit what students need to do to acquire the knowledge outlined in the learning intention.

How to effectively use learning intentions

While learning intentions and success criteria are ubiquitous in education, they are not always effectively used. Most schools will expect teachers to display and share the learning intentions for each lesson with their students. But simply sharing the learning intentions does not mean they are understood.

Help your students understand learning intentions and success criteria by using clear language, showing students what success looks like and deploying check for understanding techniques.

If the learning intentions and success criteria contain unfamiliar language, students will be unlikely to

CHAPTER
CURRICULUM & ASSESSMENT

34 CURRICULUM KNOWLEDGE | 35 FORMATIVE ASSESSMENT | **36 LEARNING INTENTIONS** | 37 CHECK FOR UNDERSTANDING PT1 |
38 CHECK FOR UNDERSTANDING PT2 | 39 GUIDED FEEDBACK | 40 COMPONENTS & COMPOSITES | 41 HOME LEARNING |
42 READING | 43 DELIBERATE VOCABULARY DEVELOPMENT | 44 TEACH TO THE TOP | 45 RESOURCE DESIGN |

understand them. Avoid using verbatim exam mark schemes and specifications. They contain too much technical language when introducing new content.

Students are more likely to be successful if they know what success looks like from the start. Give students examples of work to analyse. Let them see good and not so good examples and have them help you define the success criteria. Doing so will also develop student agency. You might need to scaffold this approach and always use check for understanding techniques to check students are getting the gist.

REFER TO **SPREAD 37 & SPREAD 38** TO READ ABOUT CHECKING FOR UNDERSTANDING.

EXAMPLES FROM PRIMARY AND SECONDARY PRACTITIONERS OF CLEAR AND CONCISE LEARNING INTENTIONS. FROM LEFT TO RIGHT AND TOP TO BOTTOM: JOHN HOUGH | LEKHA SHARMA | LOUISE CASS | EMMA TURNER.

Using big questions

Using big questions is another technique for implementing learning intentions. Big questions are posed at the beginning of a sequence of learning. At the end of the series of lessons, students answer the question. Big questions can be motivating as students see each lesson as a quest to acquire the knowledge needed to answer the overarching enquiry question. Referring back to the big question during the learning sequence can help students connect ideas and concepts into a coherent narrative. Try supplementing the big question with a series of sub-questions. You can devise these with your students at the beginning and during the learning sequence. Using sub-questions can help scaffold learning and provide success criteria for when students are ready to attempt the enquiry question.

SPREAD

37

CHECK FOR UNDERSTANDING PT1

Checking for understanding will tell you if it is safe to move on – check students' fluency before teaching new content.

What does it mean?

LEARNING IS MESSY, SO WE SHOULDN'T EXPECT EVERY STUDENT TO BE AT THE SAME POINT ALL THE TIME.

REFER TO **SPREAD 23** TO LEARN ABOUT COGNITIVE LOAD THEORY AND SCHEMAS.

Checking for understanding will be one of the most important strategies you use throughout your teaching career. Think of it as a pit stop during your lesson that allows you to see if students are grasping what you are teaching. The number of times you go through this process will vary, and there is no magic number you should be aiming for in your lesson. However, plan to do so more than once, and you don't need to stop the lesson to do it. There are multiple ways you can check for understanding, either as a whole class or with individual students.

Taught vs understood

One common misconception is the difference between students being taught new knowledge and students actually learning it. Avoid the trap of 'I've taught it, so they must have learned it' or 'I've taught it, so I don't need to go over it again'. As you teach your curriculum, there will be knowledge that you will need to revisit to build and strengthen your students' schemas because some concepts are more difficult for students to grasp. Build this into your planning. When you do your checks, you will uncover any hidden misconceptions, and you can respond to address them.

Barak Rosenshine

MORE EFFECTIVE TEACHERS FREQUENTLY CHECKED IF STUDENTS WERE LEARNING THE NEW MATERIAL.

Avoiding the pitfalls

Checking for understanding is a powerful strategy, but at the same time it can be overlooked and poorly executed. Consider the following scenario.

Annabel has been teaching her Year 7 class how to calculate the area of a circle. After explaining and modelling how to do this, Annabel says:

Does that make sense? Does anyone have any questions?

Excellent, let's get on with the questions.

| 1 | → | 2 | → | 3 | → | 4 | → | 5 | → | 6 |

CHAPTER
CURRICULUM & ASSESSMENT

34 CURRICULUM KNOWLEDGE | 35 FORMATIVE ASSESSMENT | 36 LEARNING INTENTIONS | **37 CHECK FOR UNDERSTANDING PT1** | 38 CHECK FOR UNDERSTANDING PT2 | 39 GUIDED FEEDBACK | 40 COMPONENTS & COMPOSITES | 41 HOME LEARNING | 42 READING | 43 DELIBERATE VOCABULARY DEVELOPMENT | 44 TEACH TO THE TOP | 45 RESOURCE DESIGN |

The problem here is that Annabel cannot be certain that all students do understand because some students may not feel confident enough to say that they need further support in front of their peers. So, all students stay quiet and struggle quietly.

One of the key strategies to check for understanding is asking lots of questions.

Teachers shouldn't be frightened to check for understanding. If approximately 80% of your students aren't getting correct answers during your check for understanding, they are not ready for independent practice. It means you have to reteach some of the content. If 80% or more have grasped the content, you can invest extra time with the few students that haven't.

Strategies to check for understanding

There are many methods of checking for understanding that we will cover in later spreads, such as Cold Call, mini-whiteboard work, Think, Pair, Share, probing questions etc. For now, here are a couple to whet your appetite.

Technique 1 – The collaborator

Just before setting students off on a task, check their understanding through Think, Pair, Share.

Technique 2 – The repeater

Before students begin a task, ask them to repeat your instructions to check they understand.

Tom Sherrington

RE-TEACHING REQUIRES BEING READY WITH ADDITIONAL EXAMPLES AND/OR THE NIMBLE SUBJECT KNOWLEDGE NEEDED TO GENERATE NEW QUESTIONS AND EXPLANATIONS SPONTANEOUSLY. (SHERRINGTON, 2021b)

LEARNING HAPPENS OVER TIME. YOU WILL NEED TO REVISIT KNOWLEDGE THAT YOU HAVE TAUGHT PREVIOUSLY.

A ROCK-CLIMBING INSTRUCTOR WOULD NOT CHECK THE SAFETY HARNESS OF ONE CLIMBER AND ASSUME EVERYONE IS SAFE TO BEGIN CLIMBING; SHE WOULD CHECK EVERYONE'S – INSPIRED BY AN ANALOGY USED BY TOM SHERRINGTON.

REFER BACK TO **SPREAD 25** TO LEARN MORE ABOUT HOW QUESTIONING CAN BE USED TO CHECK FOR UNDERSTANDING.

Explain to your peer what you understand about x... Be prepared to share your ideas with the rest of the class.

Tom, can you explain to the rest of the class my instructions for this task?

CHECK FOR UNDERSTANDING PT2

You know the guiding principles; now learn the techniques to check for understanding.

➕

What to do when a student says 'I don't know'

YOU CAN USE NO OPT OUT AS A BOLT-ON TO THE OTHER CHECK FOR UNDERSTANDING TECHNIQUES.

Use No Opt Out when students genuinely don't know an answer to a question or when you suspect a student is using 'I don't know' as an excuse not to think hard. When you get an 'I don't know' answer, select other students to answer the question. If multiple students cannot answer the question, it indicates you might need to reteach the content.

➕

NO OPT OUT WILL LIKELY BOOST YOUR STUDENTS' ATTENTIONAL HABITS TOO.

If you get a good answer, go back to the student(s) who claimed not to know and instruct them to repeat, rephrase or re-explain the answer. You can also use this strategy to develop the quality of a student's responses. When a student gives you a partially correct or complete answer, ask their peers to improve or add to it. Again, go back to the original student and direct them to repeat, rephrase or re-explain.

Cold Call

Cold Calling is a questioning technique to get all students thinking hard. Don't permit hands up and strategically sample student responses. As with all checking for

"Ok, it's Cold Call time. Laura, what is the capital of Australia?"

Who's doing the thinking? | Whole Class ——————→ | Just Laura

"Ok, it's Cold Call time. What is the capital of Australia...Laura?"

Who's doing the thinking? | Whole Class ————————————————→ | Just Laura

⬆

THE DIAGRAM ABOVE, ADOPTED FROM LUKE TAYLER, ILLUSTRATES WHEN TO REVEAL WHO YOU WANT TO ANSWER THE QUESTION DURING COLD CALL.

understanding techniques, don't be frightened if students get the answer wrong. If most students are getting correct answers, you know it is safe to move on; if they aren't, find out why and consider reteaching the content.

Establish routines for Cold Calling. For example, 'Okay, class, it's Cold Call time' signals all students need to think,

1 ▶ 2 ▶ 3 ▶ 4 ▶ 5 ▶ 6

CHAPTER
CURRICULUM & ASSESSMENT

34 CURRICULUM KNOWLEDGE |35 FORMATIVE ASSESSMENT | 36 LEARNING INTENTIONS | 37 CHECK FOR UNDERSTANDING PT1 |
38 CHECK FOR UNDERSTANDING PT2 | 39 GUIDED FEEDBACK | 40 COMPONENTS & COMPOSITES | 41 HOME LEARNING |
42 READING | 43 DELIBERATE VOCABULARY DEVELOPMENT | 44 TEACH TO THE TOP | 45 RESOURCE DESIGN |

as you will call on any of them to answer the question. To ensure all students are thinking about the question, provide thinking time and follow the sequence: question, pause, name. If you were to name the student before allowing thinking time, the chances are a lot of students will check out.

Mini whiteboards

Mini whiteboards are so effective as they allow you to see what every student is thinking. The teacher gets feedback about how well students are grasping the content and whether or not they are ready to practise independently.

Adam Boxer

🗩

WHEN I USE MINI WHITEBOARDS, I HAVE A MUCH BETTER CHANCE THAT STUDENTS ARE WRITING, THINKING AND DOING, EVEN IF I AM NOT GOING TO READ EVERYONE'S.
(BOXER, 2022)

It might be unrealistic to sample every answer for a large group or when the question you pose requires more than two sentences. But you'll instantly get to see who has been thinking and who has attempted to answer the question. When you can't sample all answers, aim to check the students most likely not to know. If they have got the answer correct, you can assume the rest of the class has too. Also, make sure all students believe you have sampled their responses even if you haven't.

Tom Sherrington

WHEN TEACHERS ONLY SELECT STUDENTS WHO VOLUNTEER AND ARE WORRIED ABOUT GETTING THROUGH THE MATERIAL, THEY TEND TO ASK LESS DEMANDING QUESTIONS IN ORDER TO KEEP GOING FORWARDS.
(SHERRINGTON, 2021b)

We recommend you establish a routine for distributing and using mini whiteboards. You might have a basket on each row containing whiteboards, pens and rubbers for each student. Also, decide on how you want your students to use the mini whiteboards. For example, you might insist on students keeping their boards face down until you signal for them to share their answers.

Think, Pair, Share

Think, Pair, Share helps students rehearse their answers with a peer before sharing them more widely with the rest of the class. Using this technique means all students get a chance to talk about the material. Begin by posing a question as if you were Cold Calling. After some thinking time, instruct students to discuss their answers with a peer. Follow up with the same routines from Cold Call.

SPREAD

39

GUIDED FEEDBACK
Giving effective feedback is essential for students to feedforward.

Feedback and feedforward

Feedback is a common feature of classrooms and is often delivered in the form of written or verbal comments. At some point in your lesson, you will give or receive feedback from your students.

John Hattie

IF FEEDBACK FALLS IN A CLASSROOM AND NO ONE HEARS IT, DID IT MAKE A SOUND? (HATTIE, 2021)

Meaningful learning is likely to occur when you issue feedback and engineer opportunities for students to act on this using feedforward tasks. The initial feedback informs students how well they performed against the learning intentions. Feedforward comments and activities provide a framework to support what needs to happen next.

The art of feedback

There are three key pillars to feedback: give | receive | action.

Giving feedback

FEEDBACK IS MOST EFFECTIVE WHEN STUDENTS KNOW THE LEARNING INTENTIONS AND WHAT SUCCESS LOOKS LIKE IN YOUR SUBJECT. (HATTIE, 2008)

The frequency and methods for giving feedback will depend on your school's policy. Many schools are moving to more efficient ways of issuing feedback. You can offer live feedback, either verbally or written, as you circulate the classroom during independent practice. Whole-class feedback aids responsive teaching, whereby the teacher samples students' work and plans feedforward tasks to address knowledge gaps and misconceptions. You are most likely to use written feedback for more summative assessment methods.

Receptive culture matters

It might seem that giving feedback to students is easy, but whether they want to receive it is a different matter. The relationships you build with students are important in the feedback process. Build a culture where you base feedback on how well students have performed against the learning intentions and give clear guidance on what they need to do next. Inform students how they will receive feedback on a piece of work in advance to reduce any anxiety they may have.

Dylan Wiliam

THE ONLY THING THAT MATTERS IS WHAT STUDENTS DO WITH [THE FEEDBACK]. (WILIAM, 2014)

It's all in the ACTION

What students do with your feedback is the most crucial part. Provide clear, granular next steps that are linked to the

1 → 2 → 3 → **4** → 5 → 6

CHAPTER
CURRICULUM & ASSESSMENT

34 CURRICULUM KNOWLEDGE |35 FORMATIVE ASSESSMENT | 36 LEARNING INTENTIONS | 37 CHECK FOR UNDERSTANDING PT1 | 38 CHECK FOR UNDERSTANDING PT2 | **39 GUIDED FEEDBACK** | 40 COMPONENTS & COMPOSITES | 41 HOME LEARNING | 42 READING | 43 DELIBERATE VOCABULARY DEVELOPMENT | 44 TEACH TO THE TOP | 45 RESOURCE DESIGN |

original success criteria and give students time to do them. Once students have worked on these next steps, create a feedforward activity that provides them with the opportunity to practise their next step but with a different example.

For feedback to be effective, it needs to be granular and achievable – avoid vague comments and remarks. For example, students will struggle to know what to do with this feedback: 'Excellent work, try to add more detail to your explanations.' However, the following makes explicit what students need to do: 'Use a quote to support your explanation. For example...'

Whole-class feedback

Whole-class feedback provides an efficient way to give feedback to students without writing the same comments on their books. Use marking codes to give feedback and direct students towards their next steps.

AN EXAMPLE OF HOW MICHAEL GIVES WHOLE-CLASS FEEDBACK.

Using the data table, how does the severity of hazards vary? - highlight here if you need to catch up	
Success Criteria **SC1**: Extract relevant information from the source. **SC2**: Explain how the severity of impacts of hazards vary. **SC3**: Link to examples you have studied. **SC4**: Make a judgement.	**Misconceptions** **M1**: Droughts can cause fatalities. **Improvements** **L1**: EXAMPLES - Extract specific data from the resources. **L2**: EXPLAIN - Say how this shows differences in the severity of hazards. - *This demonstrates differences in the severity of hazards because...* **L3**: COMPARE - Make a clear comparison between different types of hazards. **L4**: LINK - Give an example based on hazards you have studied.
Praise/shoutouts Excellent extraction of data from the table Clear attempts to make comparisons	**SPaG + Vocabulary Upgrade** Table | Occur *I think that = The evidence suggests that...* *Quite a lot = Expensive* 

COMPONENTS & COMPOSITES

A curriculum outlines the multifaceted outcomes encompassing both the knowledge and skills you want students to learn.

Curriculum

The curriculum is *what* is taught and not *how* it is taught. It is a carefully arranged map of what we want our students to know.

CURRICULUM	TEACHING ACTIVITIES	ASSESSMENT
WHAT IS TAUGHT.	HOW CURRICULUM CONTENT IS TAUGHT.	DESIRED HIGH-LEVEL OUTCOMES AND MEASURES OF THOSE OUTCOMES.

A well-thought-out curriculum has the following key features:

- Ambitious for all students.

- Coherently planned and sequenced.

Amanda Spielman

- Successfully adapted, designed and developed for students with special educational needs and/or disabilities.

- Broad and balanced for all students.

A GREAT CURRICULUM NEEDS TO BE BROUGHT TO LIFE, WITH GREAT TEACHING.

When teaching your curriculum, students are working towards reaching different destinations along their learning journey, called 'composites'. These composites can be multilayered encompassing layers of complex knowledge and skills. The steps your students will need to take to reach these different composites are known as the components. When considering the components that make up these more complex composites, we need to consider how they are sequenced so that we can build on prior knowledge and skills.

CHAPTER
CURRICULUM & ASSESSMENT

34 CURRICULUM KNOWLEDGE |35 FORMATIVE ASSESSMENT | 36 LEARNING INTENTIONS | 37 CHECK FOR UNDERSTANDING PT1 | 38 CHECK FOR UNDERSTANDING PT2 | 39 GUIDED FEEDBACK | **40 COMPONENTS & COMPOSITES** | 41 HOME LEARNING | 42 READING | 43 DELIBERATE VOCABULARY DEVELOPMENT | 44 TEACH TO THE TOP | 45 RESOURCE DESIGN |

An example of composite and components in art

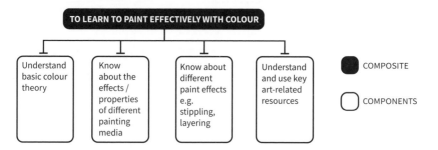

An example of composite and components in geography

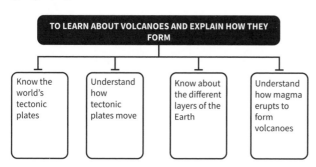

HOME LEARNING

Homework can improve student progress and boost their independence. But there are many pitfalls to consider to get it right.

Evidence about homework contradicts students' and teachers' perceptions

There is a mismatch between what the research says about homework and students' and teachers' perceptions about homework. Surveys suggest students and teachers don't think homework is beneficial to student learning. But evidence points to many advantages of students learning at home. Students are likely to perform better in exams when they complete regular homework. Plus, the EEF (2021) says home learning can add over five months to students' attainment with low-cost implications. These findings point to issues around schools' homework policies and implementation. In this spread, we aim to give you practical advice on how to get the most out of home learning and how to implement it effectively.

Rubén Fernández-Alonso, Javier Suárez-Álvarez & José Muñiz

> *OUR DATA SENDS A CLEAR MESSAGE TO TEACHING PROFESSIONALS: WELL USED, HOMEWORK REMAINS A VITAL TOOL FOR COMPREHENSIVE EDUCATION OF ADOLESCENTS.*

Why teachers and schools get homework wrong

Homework is likely to be ineffective if students need to access an online resource but can't do so. The pandemic has further exposed child poverty. Some students might have no internet access or live in a home where they share a computer with multiple siblings. If you want your students to complete homework, you need to ensure they have access to the materials they will need. When students need to use online platforms like Seneca and Carousel Learning, ensure students have login details.

| 1 | → | 2 | → | 3 | → | **4** | → | 5 | → | 6 |

CHAPTER
CURRICULUM & ASSESSMENT

34 CURRICULUM KNOWLEDGE |35 FORMATIVE ASSESSMENT | 36 LEARNING INTENTIONS |37 CHECK FOR UNDERSTANDING PT1 |
38 CHECK FOR UNDERSTANDING PT2 | 39 GUIDED FEEDBACK | 40 COMPONENTS & COMPOSITES | **41 HOME LEARNING** |
42 READING | 43 DELIBERATE VOCABULARY DEVELOPMENT | 44 TEACH TO THE TOP | 45 RESOURCE DESIGN |

If they don't have internet or computer access, provide them with printed materials. It is also worth considering the level of challenge. Homework that is challenging to access or covers unfamiliar content will likely cause students to give up. We are not suggesting you lower your expectations and standards. But the research states that when homework connects with what is happening in the lesson, and the curriculum, it yields better results. Therefore, avoid setting home learning that covers new content. Without you there to explain, model, and check for understanding, students will become overwhelmed and give up.

When planning homework, think carefully about what you intend for students to learn and communicate this to students. It is worth investing time in modelling how to complete tasks and providing students with exemplar material. Avoid setting homework for the sake of it or gimmicks. For example, building a rainforest model will likely enthuse students, but the chances are students will recall the construction of the model and not what you intended for them to learn.

When thinking about why teachers and schools get homework wrong, it seems reasonable to suggest the best kind of homework is students doing shed loads of practice. Directing students to complete knowledge retrieval activities will reduce teacher workload, help students consolidate their learning, and connect with what is happening in the classroom. On top of this, many retrieval activities are easily self- and peer-assessed, reducing teacher marking and boosting student independence.

REFER TO **SPREAD 28** TO REMIND YOURSELF ABOUT RETRIEVAL PRACTICE.

Many schools now use knowledge organisers and/or knowledge quizzes. Implementing these as homework tasks will give students an extra dose of retrieval practice. Also, it will mean students are not spending excessive hours completing homework. They will have more time to enjoy their hobbies and extracurricular activities.

SPREAD

42

READING

At the heart of an ambitious knowledge-rich curriculum is an intentional effort to help students read.

James & Dianne Murphy

TO READ IS TO HAVE ACCESS TO THE STORE OF HUMAN KNOWLEDGE. IN READING WE ENCOUNTER NOT JUST KNOWLEDGE, BUT THE MIND THAT RECORDED IT, WITH ITS EXPERIENCES AND BIASES, ITS INSIGHTS AND PERCEPTIONS.

Why reading is every teachers' responsibility

Students need to know approximately 15,000–20,000 words at the end of secondary school. Beyond the 6000 most common words in the English language, the great majority of less frequent words are more likely to be encountered in print. Suffice to say, most subject disciplines and teachers have a role in improving students' reading fluency.

Reading transmits culture and nourishes the mind. Having a firm grasp of the English language will boost students' academic success as having a vast lexicon to call on can help them express their thoughts more clearly. And yet, most teachers shy away from teaching students to read in their subject.

Teachers are likely to give up teaching students to read in their subject because it is hard to teach. They might believe it is the responsibility of the English faculty or literacy coordinator. And more unacceptable than the last two excuses: 'There is too much content to cover without adding reading to the curriculum.' Providing opportunities for students to read should be a priority for most teachers and subjects in all phases.

If you think we are stretching the truth, consider the following findings of the National Literacy Trust (see Murphy & Murphy, 2018). There are currently an estimated 6 million adults that cannot read. Poor readers are more likely to have low self-esteem and mental health issues and be victims of bullying. Given that 70% of the UK prison population cannot read, it is not an exaggeration to say the teaching profession has a moral duty to prioritise reading.

Reading should be central to curriculum planning for all the reasons we have outlined. Also, it is worth noting that reading is domain-specific. For example, reading an academic science paper is different to reading a novel in

1 → 2 → 3 → **4** → 5 → 6

CHAPTER
CURRICULUM & ASSESSMENT

34 CURRICULUM KNOWLEDGE | 35 FORMATIVE ASSESSMENT | 36 LEARNING INTENTIONS | 37 CHECK FOR UNDERSTANDING PT1 |
38 CHECK FOR UNDERSTANDING PT2 | 39 GUIDED FEEDBACK | 40 COMPONENTS & COMPOSITES | 41 HOME LEARNING |
42 READING | 43 DELIBERATE VOCABULARY DEVELOPMENT | 44 TEACH TO THE TOP | 45 RESOURCE DESIGN |

English literature. Here are some strategies to help increase your students' reading opportunities.

How did we learn before PowerPoint?

Tom Sherrington suggests one of the simplest methods to get students to read more is to park the PowerPoint addition. Teachers have become too dependent on their slides. It's as if there is no better way for students to encounter knowledge. All too often, teachers' slides contain amateur graphics and are too difficult to read at the back of the classroom. On top of this, teachers' spoken explanations are transient. Sherrington says consider where you can mix things up, presenting knowledge via printed text instead of slides.

Tom Sherrington

REVIEW YOUR POWERPOINT ADDICTION! WHERE COULD YOU SWITCH AND MIX THINGS UP SO THAT STUDENTS ARE GIVEN TEXT TO READ INSTEAD?
(SHERRINGTON, 2022)

Mary Myatt says students should have access to authentic texts about their pay grade. Teachers should scaffold to help students read demanding texts; this does not mean dumbing the content down. Instead, teachers should model reading by reading aloud, chunk sophisticated text to not overload students' working memory and provide opportunities for deliberate vocabulary development.

Mary Myatt

...THE LEARNING OF CONCEPTS AND NEW WORDS EFFICIENTLY IS BEST SERVED BY READING ALOUD TO CHILDREN TOGETHER WITH CLASSROOM DISCUSSION.
(MYATT, 2021)

When selecting texts to read, make sure they are from credible sources. Invest time in reading the material before the lesson, highlighting the unfamiliar dense noun phrases you need to emphasise for students to access the text. Consider pre-teaching these words. You will find strategies for teaching vocabulary development on the next spread.

Echo reading, a strategy suggested by Alex Quigley, helps develop students' reading fluency. The technique works by the teacher reading a passage of text, followed by her student(s). Hearing an expert read will likely improve students' fluency, and the repetitive nature of the task helps consolidate their understanding of the content.

Alex Quigley

AUTOMATIC AND FLUENT READING IS ESSENTIAL FOR STUDENTS TO CONCENTRATE THEIR WORKING MEMORY RESOURCES ON THE COMPLEXITY OF THE TEXT.
(QUIGLEY, 2021)

DELIBERATE VOCABULARY DEVELOPMENT

Students with broad and rich vocabularies will learn more, remember more and be able to access a rich and demanding curriculum.

Reading and vocabulary development can and should be mutually reinforcing

Mary Myatt

Reading and vocabulary development can and should be mutually reinforcing. Students should, where possible, encounter domain-specific vocabulary in the texts you require them to read. Equally, students need a grasp of technical language to make meaning from text. Therefore, students need a mixed diet of deliberate vocabulary development. Here are some strategies to get you going.

THE CONCEPTS AND BIG IDEAS ARE GENERALLY TIER THREE VOCABULARY. THEY ARE THE GATEWAYS INTO THE INDIVIDUAL SUBJECTS. IF WE WANT PUPILS TO KNOW MORE AND REMEMBER MORE, IT'S WORTH SPENDING TIME TEACHING THEM, TALKING ABOUT THEM, AND SHOWING THEM IN LOTS OF DIFFERENT CONTEXTS. (MYATT, 2022a)

🔟 Tiers of vocabulary

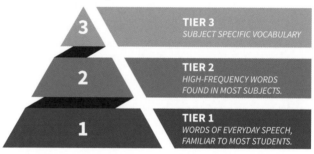

Use tiers of vocabulary to identify the words and phrases you need to teach. Invest time developing students' understanding and fluency of tier 2 and tier 3 words by engineering opportunities for students to read, write and say the words. A word of caution: tier 2 words can be a false friend. They frequently appear in multiple disciplines but often have a different meaning in those subjects. It pays to explicitly teach all tier 2 and tier 3 words through the lens of your domain and not leave students' understanding to chance.

Have students practise saying words to build their fluency

Building students' fluency in using sophisticated vocabulary requires practice. Provide opportunities for students to say the words they need to know. Choral responses are when the whole class or a group of students

CHAPTER
CURRICULUM & ASSESSMENT

34 CURRICULUM KNOWLEDGE | 35 FORMATIVE ASSESSMENT | 36 LEARNING INTENTIONS | 37 CHECK FOR UNDERSTANDING PT1 |
38 CHECK FOR UNDERSTANDING PT2 | 39 GUIDED FEEDBACK | 40 COMPONENTS & COMPOSITES | 41 HOME LEARNING |
42 READING | **43 DELIBERATE VOCABULARY DEVELOPMENT** | 44 TEACH TO THE TOP | 45 RESOURCE DESIGN |

say words simultaneously. Begin by having all students say a word chorally. To ensure all students build fluency, follow up by directing individual rows or groups and then individual students to say the words. Using choral responses is an effective method for developing students' pronunciation of complex vocabulary.

Another strategy we have found to be effective is to activate students as a learning resource for one another. In pairs, students discuss the meaning of the words they are learning. To make this meaningful, provide structured questions that force students to use the to-be-learned words. Display the questions on a whiteboard (or equivalent device) or print them. The questions could include: 'What does ... mean?' or 'Can you use the word ... in a sentence?' or 'Where else might you use this word?' or 'Can you think of a different word that has the same meaning?' This technique works because it allows you to circulate the room. As you survey the classroom, identify errors or misconceptions and ensure discussions remain focused.

Etymology can unlock the meaning of words

As well as being profoundly interesting, etymology and morphology allow students to develop their lexicon through observing patterns. Many tier 3 words students use have ancient Greek and Latin origins. Rather helpfully, many of these words contain common word roots (hydro, bio, geo), prefixes (anti-, mono-, micro-) and suffixes (-graphy, -ology, -ing, -ed). Making the origins of a word explicit can help memorably explain concepts. For example, when introducing students to the concept of a biome, the teacher could explain how the word contains the Greek root *bíos*, meaning life and the Latin suffix -ome, meaning a collection. The teacher would then explain how a biome is a collection or community of living things. To make explicit to your students the common patterns within tier 3 vocabulary, direct them to construct words by matching roots, prefixes and suffixes.

Alex Quigley

WHEN YOU EXPLORE THE HISTORY AND ROOTS OF A WORD – THE ETYMOLOGY – YOU DRAW UPON A RICH STORY THAT CAN UNLOCK UNDERSTANDING FOR OUR PUPILS IN SCIENCE, MATHS, GEOGRAPHY, AND MORE. IT CAN ADD A LAYER OF UNDERSTANDING THAT HELPS OUR NOVICE PUPILS HOOK INTO A TRICKY ACADEMIC TERM THAT MAY HAVE REMAINED ABSTRACT AND INSCRUTABLE TO THEM. (QUIGLEY, 2020)

TEACH TO THE TOP

Students have the right to a demanding and challenging curriculum; a curriculum that does not limit what they can learn and how far they can go.

Teaching to the top benefits all students

Students should not have limits imposed on their learning. If all you expect of your students is low-level responses, all you will get are low-level responses. To borrow a line from Sam Strickland: you permit what you promote and promote what you permit.

Mary Myatt

PUPILS THEMSELVES ARE SAYING THAT THEY ENJOY DOING DEMANDING WORK, SO LET'S NOT PUT LIMITS ON THEIR LEARNING, AND LET'S REMIND OURSELVES THAT IN THE SCHOOL INSPECTION HANDBOOK IT SAYS THAT WE SHOULD BE OFFERING A CURRICULUM THAT IS 'AMBITIOUS FOR ALL PUPILS, PARTICULARLY DISADVANTAGED PUPILS AND INCLUDING PUPILS WITH SEND.' (MYATT, 2022b)

Most classes are 'mixed-ability'. Teaching to the top, and scaffolding for those needing it, ensures all students benefit. Top-performing students feel valued as capable thinkers, and those needing additional support encounter more challenging content than if you were to 'dumb down' your questions, resources and learning intentions.

In most settings, gone are the days where teachers 'differentiate by outcomes', providing students in the same class with different work because a spreadsheet dictates how far they can go. It is fair to say this is morally wrong, demotivates students and adds to teachers' workload. Plus, the Ofsted Framework, the Early Career Framework and the Teachers' Standards all speak of the need for teachers to be setting audacious goals.

Teachers with high academic expectations do not consider learning done when students answer questions correctly. They see this as an opportunity to go even further; their students are self-confident and curious, and the classroom culture builds on the notion that learning is never complete. These teachers select the most demanding curriculum options, including texts and activities, and pose the most challenging questions.

Curriculum implications

While you might not be the gatekeeper of the curriculum as a new teacher, you have a seat at the table. Along with your colleagues, you should identify and enact the most challenging curriculum options. Teachers should prioritise depth over speed. Avoid shallow learning and racing through your slides because you need to 'deliver the content'.

| 1 | → | 2 | → | 3 | → | 4 | → | 5 | → | 6 |

CHAPTER
CURRICULUM & ASSESSMENT

34 CURRICULUM KNOWLEDGE |35 FORMATIVE ASSESSMENT | 36 LEARNING INTENTIONS | 37 CHECK FOR UNDERSTANDING PT1 | 38 CHECK FOR UNDERSTANDING PT2 | 39 GUIDED FEEDBACK | 40 COMPONENTS & COMPOSITES | 41 HOME LEARNING | 42 READING | 43 DELIBERATE VOCABULARY DEVELOPMENT | **44 TEACH TO THE TOP** | 45 RESOURCE DESIGN |

It pays to agree on what excellence looks like in your faculty. First, identify the big ideas and the key strands underpinning your domain or phase. For each of these, discuss what you would expect a top-performing student to be able to do at the end of each key stage. You and your faculty can then create exemplar work and success criteria around these expectations.

Tom Sherrington

CELEBRATE INTELLECTUAL CURIOSITY ... MAKE IT NORMAL TO DO THINGS THAT ARE DIFFICULT AND ACADEMIC [IN NATURE]. (SHERRINGTON, 2017)

It also pays to explore how your subject evolves through each key stage; if you are a KS2 teacher, find out what your students will learn during KS3, and so on. In KS3, you might explore how you can incorporate key concepts from KS4. However, a word of caution: we are not suggesting you begin teaching GCSE specifications in KS3 or asking GCSE-style questions in Year 7. As your subject progresses, the concepts will become more challenging, and students will likely need to make more connections across topics. Exploring how your domain evolves will help you help your students prepare for the extended demands they will face.

Another strategy is to plan for students to redraft their work. Having students do this is an intentional move beyond accepting mediocrity. It provides students with evidence that they are capable of creating beautiful work. It would be unrealistic to have students redraft every piece of work they do. But along with your colleagues, identify a few demanding tasks throughout the year where students can refine and improve their work, supported by effective feedback.

Doug Lemov

IN THE CLASSROOMS WITH THE HIGHEST ACADEMIC EXPECTATIONS, RIGHT ANSWERS AREN'T THE END OF THE LEARNING PROCESS; INSTEAD, THEY OPEN THE DOOR TO FURTHER CHALLENGE. (LEMOV, 2021)

Get forensic with your questioning

Show your students you care about what they think by asking follow-up questions, even if they have given you a correct answer. Doing so will reveal your students' understanding while developing their schema. There will be times when students correctly answer a question, but they arrive at their response by fluke. The only way to truly unearth what they know is to follow up their initial answer with further questions, such as, 'How are A and B similar or different? What other examples support your argument?'

SPREAD

45

RESOURCE DESIGN
Despite their obvious benefits, most teachers aren't taught how to design resources.

Why your resources matter

Oliver Caviglioli

THE UNDERSTANDABLE YET FUNDAMENTALLY MISTAKEN ASSUMPTION OF TEACHERS TO BE ARTISTIC BY INTRODUCING WHAT APPEARS TO BE A RANDOM PLACEMENT OF ELEMENTS ON A PAGE IS A MAJOR HANDICAP IN THEIR COMMUNICATION EFFECTIVENESS.

Teachers spend hours designing resources. Creating resources allows teachers to tailor them to their curriculum and the needs of their students. It seems reasonable to assert that many teachers enjoy producing their own materials, and some will argue it helps develop their subject knowledge. But most teachers have little-to-no understanding or experience of design principles. It is not their fault. Our profession recognises cognitive load theory as being the single most important thing for teachers to know, but negates an area filled with opportunities to disobey the principles of this theory.

Curb your enthusiasm

Alberto Cairo

...STICK TO JUST TWO OR THREE COLORS AND PLAY WITH THEIR SHADES.

DO THE SAME WITH FONTS. CHOOSE JUST ONE OR TWO: A SOLID, THICK ONE FOR HEADLINES, AND A READABLE ONE FOR BODY COPY.

Despite having access to information at our fingertips, newspapers and magazines remain popular. Their ability to communicate information with immeasurable clarity has to be a contributing factor. So if you want to get better at designing resources, study broadsheet newspapers and news magazines, such as *The Economist* and *The Guardian Weekly*.

To enhance your work, resist the temptation to use too much colour and fancy fonts. Restrict your designs to two or three colours where possible. If you need to use colour to signal a key, use a small, subtle graphic element such as a square or rectangle. Also, avoid having large amounts of text on top of colour boxes. Stick to black and white to make the text more readable.

Fancy fonts will not make the content of your lesson more engaging and will likely hinder students' ability to read it. Many teachers resort to using Comic Sans as it is dyslexia-friendly. However, it is worth noting that the British Dyslexia Association recommend several other fonts that are equally beneficial and less gimmicky: Arial, Verdana, Tahoma, Century Gothic, Trebuchet and Calibri. We suggest using no more than two fonts per design, one a san serif and the other a serif.

1 → 2 → 3 → **4** → 5 → 6

CHAPTER
CURRICULUM & ASSESSMENT

34 CURRICULUM KNOWLEDGE | 35 FORMATIVE ASSESSMENT | 36 LEARNING INTENTIONS | 37 CHECK FOR UNDERSTANDING PT1 | 38 CHECK FOR UNDERSTANDING PT2 | 39 GUIDED FEEDBACK | 40 COMPONENTS & COMPOSITES | 41 HOME LEARNING | 42 READING | 43 DELIBERATE VOCABULARY DEVELOPMENT | 44 TEACH TO THE TOP | **45 RESOURCE DESIGN**

While you might expect your students to underline the titles in their exercise books, you don't have to in your designs. During the age of the typewriter, there was no other way of denoting the title other than underlining it. The same is true of students' exercise books. But with your creations, you can adjust the thickness of a title, colour and font.

Take out your Ockham's razor

Ockham's razor is a principle that describes how, by removing unnecessary information, we arrive at the truth or a better explanation sooner. Applying this rule to your resources means reducing the extraneous load – cull any graphic or text that does not strengthen students' understanding of the content.

Let the page breathe

Behind all magazines and newspapers is a grid. It is invisible to the untrained eye but enhances publishers' communication abilities. Grids allow you to neatly align your work and reduce the chances of your designs becoming overly cluttered. Most software has a grid or guide function. Even Microsoft Word now boasts this feature. You can find tutorials on YouTube to get you going. Once you have designed a grid, you have a template for all your designs.

A brief glance at the grids below should demonstrate the versatility and professional touch they afford.

THE SAME PRINCIPLES APPLY TO YOUR SLIDES. A GOOD LITMUS TEST IS TO SIT AS FAR AWAY FROM YOUR BOARD AS POSSIBLE; IF YOU CAN'T READ THE TEXT ON YOUR SLIDES, YOUR STUDENTS WON'T BE ABLE TO EITHER.

Ruth Clark & Richard Mayer

OUR SINGLE MOST IMPORTANT RECOMMENDATION IS TO KEEP THE LESSON UNCLUTTERED. IN SHORT, ACCORDING TO THE COHERENCE PRINCIPLE, YOU SHOULD AVOID ADDING ANY MATERIAL THAT DOES NOT SUPPORT THE INSTRUCTIONAL GOAL.

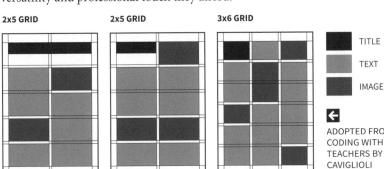

2x5 GRID   **2x5 GRID**   **3x6 GRID**

TITLE

TEXT

IMAGE

ADOPTED FROM DUAL CODING WITH TEACHERS BY OLIVER CAVIGLIOLI

PASTORAL

05

50

PSHE
PSHE is an
essential part of
the curriculum,
covering a broad
range of complex
issues.

51

ENRICHMENT
Enrichment can
give students
culturally rounded
experiences,
enhancing their
learning and
broadening their
horizons.

BEING A FORM TUTOR

You are likely to see the students in your form more frequently than any other group, so establishing routines and culture is vital.

Molly McDonough
Head of geography

EACH SCHOOL HAS A DIFFERENT APPROACH TO BEING A FORM TUTOR. FOR SOME, YOU MAY BE THE PRIMARY PASTORAL LEAD; FOR OTHERS, PART OF A WIDER HOUSE OR YEAR GROUP TEAM.

Being a form tutor is a wonderful experience and an opportunity to establish strong relationships between students, home and school.

Having clear expectations and consistent routines allows for students to thrive

High expectations are vital as it is likely that the relationship with your tutees will be different to the one you have with your teaching groups, as you are undertaking a pastoral role; however, it is important that your expectations remain the same. Ensure these are clear to tutees and uphold your classroom values as normal by following the behaviour policy.

To support these high expectations, have consistent routines with your form group. Each day of the week, have a set activity so both you and your students know what to expect. This helps build the culture of your form but also allows you to carve out time to intervene or mentor students as both routines and expectations are concrete.

Building strong channels of communication

There are three important strands of communication to establish regarding your tutor group. Firstly, being a form tutor gives you the gift of time to get to know your tutor group, more than you may get with teaching groups. Use this time to discover the hobbies, interests and passions of your tutor group. Secondly, building relationships with home is vital to support your tutees. Sending an email introducing yourself sets a positive tone to these relationships; furthermore, emailing or phoning with praise can strengthen this connection. Established relationships also make difficult conversations easier as there is an existing rapport between home and school.

Tom Bennett

ROUTINES ARE THE BUILDING BLOCKS OF THE CLASSROOM CULTURE. ROUTINE BEHAVIOUR MUST BE TAUGHT AND NOT TOLD.
(BENNETT, 2020a)

Lastly, communication with class teachers. As their form tutor, you have oversight of students both pastorally and academically, often being the member of staff who can grasp the 'big picture'. Speaking to your tutees' class

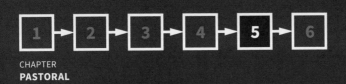
teachers allows you to build this picture and best investigate any concerns you, the student or those at home might have.

Creating a culture of success and achievement helps create form pride

Many schools have house or form competitions throughout the year. Participation in these builds pride within your form as it creates a sense of belonging and helps students to work collaboratively. Furthermore, celebrate their achievements both inside and outside of the classroom; knowing that you care and are celebrating their achievements with them helps foster strong relationships with your tutees.

CONSIDER HOW YOU CAN CELEBRATE SUCCESS IN YOUR FORM SUCH AS TOP HOUSE POINTS, RANDOM ACTS OF KINDNESS AND VOTES FOR FORM MEMBER OF THE TERM.

Safeguarding your tutor group

Although safeguarding your tutor group is not your sole responsibility, you will see them more than other staff. Here are three core ideas – the ABC – to look out for with your tutees:

Attendance: You are likely to be the only member of staff who registers the students everyday. Look for trends in attendance such as absences on a particular day, lateness and prolonged absences.

Behaviour: Review students' behaviour, both positively and negatively, in lessons and around the school. Identifying trends allows you to intervene if necessary, engage in mentoring with these students and praise or challenge accordingly.

Character: Knowing your tutees well will allow you to identify changes in their character. This can be for many reasons, including simply growing up, but can also be an indicator of something else.

PARENTS' EVENING

Parental engagement is an important factor in supporting students' progress.

Parental engagement

During your training year, you will have an opportunity to engage with parents through several different methods: phone calls, 1:1 meetings, emails, and parents' evenings.

SEE **SPREAD 48** TO LEARN MORE ABOUT PARENT PHONE CALLS.

Each provides you with an opportunity to share with parents their child's success and areas for improvement within your subject. The format of parents' evenings will depend on your school but despite this difference, making contact throughout the academic year is important to build engagement with parents.

Parent evening myths

MYTH 1 – *Parents' evenings are an ideal opportunity to inform parents that their child is not behaving in your lessons.*

If you leave this until parents' evening, it will lead to a counterproductive conversation. Use other forms of communication throughout the academic year to work on strategies together.

MYTH 2 – *Parents' evenings require you to remember each one of your students from memory.*

After a day of teaching, it would be a challenge to remember everything about each of your students. Be prepared with what you want to say.

TO LEARN MORE ABOUT PARENTAL ENGAGEMENT, READ THE EEF REPORT HERE – HTTPS:// EDUCATION ENDOWMENT FOUNDATION.ORG.UK/ EDUCATION-EVIDENCE/ TEACHING-LEARNING-TOOLKIT/PARENTAL-ENGAGEMENT

Parents' evening tips

TIP 1 – *Be prepared with the key information about your students to share with parents.*

TIP 2 – *Plan a brief overview of some key points you want to share with parents about their child.*

TIP 3 – *Bring a year seating plan with student photos. Especially useful if you have just begun at the school or recently inherited the class.*

TIP 4 – *Keep to time by front-loading your introduction with how long the meeting will take.*

Using the GROW model for parental conversations

In preparation for your parental conversations, use the GROW model. This will allow you to focus the conversation on communicating what their child needs to do to improve.

GOAL

Outline the aspirations for their child within your subject. For example, identify a specific area that would enable them to move forward.

REALITY

What are the obstacles for their child to achieve the goal? For example, behaviour for learning, completion of homework, or knowledge gaps.

OPTIONS

Outline what their child needs to do to overcome the obstacles you have discussed above.

WAY FORWARD

Set targets for the next few weeks and provide parents with the tools to support their child with them at home.

John Hattie

THE EFFECT OF PARENTAL ENGAGEMENT OVER A STUDENT'S SCHOOL CAREER IS EQUIVALENT TO ADDING TWO OR THREE YEARS TO THAT STUDENT'S EDUCATION. (HATTIE, 2008)

SPREAD

48

PARENT PHONE CALLS

In most cases, parents are the most influential factor in your students' lives – build a rapport with parents so they can help you help their child.

Most students are shaped by their parents – context is key

Parents are arguably the biggest influence in a child's life. In most cases, parents want the best for their child. Therefore, building alliances with parents should be something you do to mitigate or remedy undesirable student behaviour.

Tom Bennett

BUT MOST PARENTS, THE MAJORITY, CARE FAR MORE DEEPLY ABOUT THEIR CHILD THAN YOU EVER WILL. ALL OF OUR COMMUNICATION MUST BE FRAMED RESPECTING THAT RELATIONSHIP BETWEEN CHILDREN AND THEIR PARENTS. (BENNETT, 2020a)

Unfortunately, some students' parents will support them through blind loyalty. A small minority will not be forthcoming with their support for the school due to, rightly or wrongly, a lack of faith in education – previous experiences cause some parents to distrust the education system. An even smaller number of parents have mental health issues and have unrealistic expectations of teachers and schools. And unfortunately, an even smaller cohort of parents physically and emotionally abuse their children.

Disarming parents' anxieties about school

Anything you can do to alleviate a parents' anxieties about education can only increase your chances of gaining their support. Don't wait for students to misbehave before contacting home. Where possible, make parent calls at the beginning of the academic year. Use this as an opportunity to tell parents how much you are looking forward to teaching their child and outline your expectations. Doing so will help change the perception that school only contacts home when there is a behavioural issue. Most parents will be pleasantly surprised by your call. And you should find that parents are more supportive if you have to call them about behaviour in the future.

FOR TEACHERS WITH MANY GROUPS, TARGET THE PARENTS OF STUDENTS YOU MIGHT NEED TO SPEAK WITH IN THE FUTURE.

Help me to help your child

Write a script before phoning parents. Doing so will increase the clarity of your communication and reduce the risk of your emotions running the conversation. When calling home, never begin the conversation by talking about negative behaviour. Try to speak about something positive, and ask if now is a convenient time to talk.

Carl Hendrick

PLEASE HELP ME TO HELP YOUR SON/DAUGHTER.

PHONING PARENTS

Purpose and context

Write a script for phoning parents. If you have to leave a voicemail, explain you wish to speak to the parent and offer a suitable time for them to call you back or when you will attempt to call back. If your school requires you to log calls, do so as soon after the call as possible; this will ensure you don't forget the main details.

1 Make the call

Introduce yourself and ask if they have the time to talk. Make small talk by saying something positive about the student, their learning and their progress in your subject.

2 Positive framing

When discussing the behavioural issue, frame it as though it is out of the ordinary. Most parents don't want to feel as though their child frequently misbehaves.

3 Help me help your child

Ask the parent to help you get their child back on track. Doing so will send the message you care about their child's learning and behaviour. Also, it signals you wish to work with them and their child.

Sam Lawrence
Assistant principal,
director of pastoral
systems

It could happen here
Safeguarding children is everyone's responsibility. Don't assume it won't happen in your school – these issues can and do happen everywhere. Since everyone has a role to play, information sharing between professionals is key. Serious Case Reviews have repeatedly shown the dangers of failing to share information and take effective action.

Knowledge is power
Find out which students in your classes are in a vulnerable category – children with SEND, 'looked after' children or children with a social worker all come under this group. Ask the designated safeguarding lead (DSL), pastoral leads or SENDCo for information about these students. Not only will this help you support them, it means you can be more vigilant to help to keep them safe from harm.

Culture
You are a key part of creating a culture of safeguarding in your school. Challenge things you see happening inside and outside of the classroom that are inappropriate. There is no such thing as banter, and normalising offensive comments can make your classroom feel unsafe for some children. Tackle this behaviour to maintain trusted relationships.

Online presence
Check your privacy settings on social media, then check them again. Settings can change with new updates and leave profiles open to public view. If a student tries to contact you on social media, inform your DSL who will advise of the best course of action.

Reporting concerns

Every school will have a designated safeguarding lead (DSL) who is part of the senior leadership team. Find out who this person is and if they have a team, who they are. Your school will have a reporting system for safeguarding concerns. If in doubt, always report any concerns. Nothing is too small to share and may help your DSL understand the bigger picture for a child. Trust your gut.

No secrets

You can NEVER promise a child confidentiality. Don't worry that sharing information may damage your relationship with the child or stop them from reporting something again – the safety of the child is paramount. Tell the child you need to share information to help keep them safe. This can provide reassurance that not everyone will find out.

Seek support

Recognise that some concerns you share may be upsetting and it is important you access support with this if needed. You can follow up on any reported concerns after a few days with your DSL. They may be unable to tell you the exact actions that have been taken but they will be able to reassure you about the next steps to support a child.

SPREAD

50

PSHE

PSHE is an essential part of the curriculum, covering a broad range of complex issues.

What is PSHE?

Personal, social, health and economic (PSHE) education is essential for students' education. The government require schools to tailor their PSHE curriculum to fit the context and reflect the needs of their students. A good PSHE curriculum will build on the school's curriculum, the national curriculum and statutory guidance on drug education, financial education, relationship and sex education and the importance of physical activity and diet for a healthy lifestyle. Relationships education is compulsory for primary schools, and relationships and sex education (RSE) is compulsory for all secondary schools.

Why PSHE matters

PSHE tackles many critical day-to-day issues students are likely to encounter: friendship issues, emotional wellbeing, change and much more. It also seeks to help students make informed choices about alcohol and drugs and give them the skills to succeed in their first job. In a nutshell, a good PSHE curriculum should equip students with the knowledge and skills to thrive in a world chock-full of challenges.

Teaching PSHE

Like any subject, PSHE is most effective when it is carefully sequenced and the knowledge builds on prior learning. Schools should dedicate at least an hour per week to PSHE. Many schools are creative with their PSHE provision to give more time to other curriculum areas. Schools will include PSHE in their tutor programme or have termly drop-down days. No matter your school's provisions, you will want to be confident in delivering a range of topics, some of which will cover complex issues.

We recommend you visit the government-funded PSHE Association. Your school is likely a member. Here you will find resources and guidance – carefully curated by phase – for planning, teaching and assessing all PSHE topics.

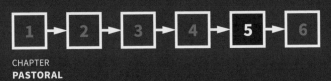
When teaching a PSHE lesson, it is best to assume at least one student in the class has been or is likely affected by the topic, given the complexity and breadth of themes covered by PSHE. Doing so will require you to consider your language use, resources and activities. From time to time, there are high-profile and controversial issues reported in the media. The key is to create a safe learning environment.

A safe learning environment should allow students to express their views and consider those of their peers. It will provide a forum for sharing feelings and exploring beliefs, values and attitudes, all while being free of negative feedback. Such an environment should encourage discussion and help the teacher feel less anxious about unexpected comments or disclosures.

ALWAYS SIGNPOST SUPPORT WITHIN THE SCHOOL AND BEYOND. EXPLAIN TO STUDENTS HOW TO SEEK SUPPORT FROM DIFFERENT SERVICES.

Establishing ground rules with your class will help create a safe learning environment. The PSHE association recommends teachers have ground rules around openness – being honest, discussing examples and not personal details of others. They suggest that teachers establish a non-judgemental culture, and students should be allowed to 'pass' if they don't feel comfortable engaging in a discussion.

As the teacher, you should be careful not to express your own views and provide access to balanced information to help students shape their opinions. You might consider having a box in your classroom where students can anonymously post questions or concerns.

Always offer an age-appropriate, factual response when faced with tricky questions. If you do not know the answer, buy yourself some time. Be honest and explain that you do not know the answer, but you will find out and share it in the next lesson. Finally, it goes without saying that if a student shares a comment or question that concerns you, you must report it to your relevant safeguarding and child protection lead.

ENRICHMENT

Enrichment can give students culturally rounded experiences, enhancing their learning and broadening their horizons.

Why enrichment matters

School enrichment seeks to develop student character, and the skills and behaviours that likely underpin school and life success. Such skills include resilience, social skills, independence and motivation. These skills can be developed inside and outside the classroom.

Your school's enrichment programme is likely to include enterprise events, cultural and sporting trips, and university visits. Enrichment opportunities are some of the most memorable and enjoyable experiences for both students and teachers. Enrichment can make subjects more meaningful, providing experiences not available in the classroom. For disadvantaged students, it provides them with opportunities and experiences they are unlikely to get outside of school.

School enrichment

School enrichment should develop students' interests and talents, enabling them to build resiliency, confidence and independence. Schools are required to teach students how to keep mentally and physically fit. And students should be taught to be responsible, respectful and active citizens prepared for future success beyond school life.

Enrichment in the classroom

In the classroom, enriching students' lives can include a diverse curriculum. As explained on spread 34, diversifying the curriculum gives students a more balanced view of the world and helps them find their place. When introducing a new concept, explore with your students its origins. For example, learning the etymology of words is not only enriching but will also lead to students expanding their vocabulary.

SEE BEN RANSON'S
WORK HERE: HTTPS://
WWW.BENRANSON.UK/
BOOKLETS

Consider how you can use diverse role models for your subjects, revealing their contributions and highlighting their importance. For example, in Ben Ranson's geography lessons, students explore the Islamic explorer Muhammad al-Idrisi's contribution to modern cartography.

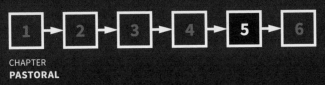

Enrichment outside of the classroom

As a trainee teacher, you will likely be enthusiastic and want to involve yourself as much as possible in all aspects of school life. But be sure to balance your teaching commitment with what you can offer outside the classroom. Consider your hobbies and interests and how they might make for an enriching experience for students. You might have an interest in something the school does not yet offer. Alternatively, there might be a club already running, and you want to be involved in it. Whatever your involvement, you will find enrichment very rewarding as your students boost their cultural capital.

Trips and visits

Trips and visits offer many benefits. Whether students are visiting a local museum or going on a ski trip abroad, trips can significantly influence students' character. Such occasions require considerable planning and therefore need mining for all their worth.

If the intention is to expand students' learning beyond the classroom, you should prepare them before the visit. Providing students with the context of what they are about to see will enhance the trip, making it more meaningful. Also, students are likely to get more from it if you design tasks that engage them in the contents of the visit and assign consolidation work when they return to the classroom.

When you go on your first school trip, you need to familiarise yourself with your school's policies. There are heightened levels of responsibility and expectation placed on you on a school trip, no matter the scale. To ensure you know what to do in an emergency or unexpected event, you must read all risk assessments and check with the trip leader if something is unclear. A well-planned trip will have a comprehensive itinerary and contingency plans for when things go awry. Familiarise yourself with all documentation; never be afraid to ask if you are unsure.

PROFESSIONAL DEVELOPMENT

06

Justin Wakefield
Vice principal

Interviews are a way of showcasing everything about you. Simply, employers will be looking to assess your knowledge, skill set, experience and capacity for growth. Rehearsing your approach via the four P structure will ensure you are better prepared for the process.

1 PRE INTERVIEW

Preparation

Use your time wisely. Invest time in researching and visiting the school. Use a variety of sources such as the school website, recent Ofsted reports and other key documentation to build a profile of the school setting. A visit to the school is a great way of gaining an initial feeling for the workplace and will be welcomed by school leaders.

Plan – School tour and student council

Write down questions that you will you ask your tour guide, making sure you link this to the ethos and values of the school. Ask questions around the Ofsted report to leaders and gain students' views on school improvement. This will be very helpful information on the day.

Plan – Teach part/full lesson

As to be expected, you will need to showcase your teaching practice to your potential employer. Prior to the day, make sure you ask for student details, seating plans (so you can use these to personalise your approach), progress data and curriculum information. Knowing the students' prior knowledge and future intent will enable you to plan and support effectively.

Plan – Formal interview

All interview questions follow standardised themes. Questions will seek to discuss your motivation for applying for the post, personal strengths and areas of development, knowledge of pedagogy, safeguarding and statutory

1 → 2 → 3 → 4 → 5 → 6

CHAPTER
PROFESSIONAL DEVELOPMENT

52 INTERVIEWS | 53 PERSONAL STATEMENTS | 54 PROFESSIONAL LEARNING | 55 TEACHER INSIGHTS | 56 THE ECF |
57 THE ECF PT2 | 58 MENTOR MEETINGS | 59 ENGAGING WITH RESEARCH | 60 GLOWING UP, NOT BURNING OUT |
61 TEACHER STUDY PT1 | 62 TEACHER STUDY PT2 | 63 TEACHER STUDY PT3 | 64 TEACHER STUDY PT4 |

guidance. Create potential questions with model answers in preparation for your rehearsal.

Practice
Regular rehearsal of your plan will ensure that this information is retained and executed on interview day. Rehearsal will give you an opportunity to delete, substitute or keep relevant information (Marzano, Pickering & Pollock, 2001).

2 INTERVIEW DAY

Perform
First impressions are vitally important in starting the process positively and setting a tone for the rest of the interview. Now is the time to use your previous planning that should be part of your long-term memory. To give a positive first impression to colleagues, you should consider:

**Janine Willis &
Alexander Todorov**
🔋

*A TENTH OF A SECOND
IS THE TIME IT TAKES TO
FORM AN IMPRESSION
OF A STRANGER FROM
EXPOSURE TO THEIR FACE.*

Attire
Dress appropriately and in line with the school's dress code.

Attendance
Be the first to arrive and last to leave. Make sure you depart from your home well in advance just in case you experience delay; no excuses, no exceptions.

Attention
Reflect on your body language regularly. Maintain good posture, smile, make eye contact, and be positive and personable at all times.

SPREAD

53

PERSONAL STATEMENTS

Personal statements are critical in providing a first
impression of you to your potential employer.

Justin Wakefield
Vice principal

BEFORE STARTING TO
DRAFT YOUR PERSONAL
STATEMENT, MAP THIS
OUT USING POST-IT
NOTES.

During your teaching career there will be lots of exciting
job and career progression opportunities that you opt to
apply for. Structuring your personal statement using the
BEST structure will ensure you increase your chances of
landing that dream interview.

Paragraph 1: Beliefs

The first part of your personal statement should be the
'hook'. Include your beliefs and motives for applying for
the role. What makes you different to the rest of the field?
Employers have your accomplishments listed on your CV;
talk about your passion for the profession, the schools'
values and why you want to teach/lead at the school.

Paragraph 2: Experience

Whether you have performed one week or one term, you
have gained experience in the profession. Talk about this.
State the many aspects of the curriculum you've delivered,
the enrichment opportunities you've supported and how
you have engaged with the parental community.

Paragraph 3: Suitability

We are all individual. What makes you *you*? Talk about the
skills and qualities that you could bring to the role without
sounding arrogant. Schools and teams are looking for
people who can add value and integrate successfully. Make
sure you link this to the job description and specification.

BE CONCISE. ENSURE
THAT YOUR PERSONAL
STATEMENT IS NO MORE
THAN TWO SIDES OF A4.

Paragraph 4: Tie together

This is your chance to leave a lasting impression on the
employer. It is crucial that you link to and summarise the
main points of your statement.

Your personal statement is an opportunity for you to
provide more depth to your CV, not to repeat it. Make sure
you celebrate your uniqueness and link this to the vision
and aims of your employer.

1 → 2 → 3 → 4 → 5 → 6

CHAPTER
PROFESSIONAL DEVELOPMENT

52 INTERVIEWS | **53 PERSONAL STATEMENTS** | 54 PROFESSIONAL LEARNING | 55 TEACHER INSIGHTS | 56 THE ECF |
57 THE ECF PT2 | 58 MENTOR MEETINGS | 59 ENGAGING WITH RESEARCH | 60 GLOWING UP, NOT BURNING OUT |
61 TEACHER STUDY PT1 | 62 TEACHER STUDY PT2 | 63 TEACHER STUDY PT3 | 64 TEACHER STUDY PT4 |

Standout statement starters

Here are some examples of starter stems within the BEST
approach.

BELIEFS	I firmly believe that teaching has the ability to inspire and positively impact on the next generation of talent. My journey into teaching started…
EXPERIENCE	My current role has cemented my firm understanding of [key stage phase] and helped me deliver and support…
SUITABILITY	I would use my initiative, positive attitude and relationships to promote the [school] values.
TIE TOGETHER	Ultimately, I feel very suited to this position; I believe I have the appropriate ethos and set of skills needed to make a difference. I consider that my humour, passion and firm resilience will help to motivate both colleagues and students.

SPREAD

54

PROFESSIONAL LEARNING

On this spread, John Hough discusses teaching concepts, and what they are and are not.

John Hough
Assistant head of secondary education

Within teaching, there are many concepts used to support our professional learning

To apply these concepts effectively to your practice, knowing their origins provides clarity on what you're trying to achieve and what you're trying to avoid. Otherwise, we might reinvent the wheel both square and round. We will discuss two such concepts – responsive and adaptive teaching – to help shape your teacher judgement.

Adaptive and responsive teaching relates to classroom decisions made by teachers to maximise the progress of students

Although thoughtful planning is key, this aspect of practice is about reading the room while using your knowledge of the students and your subject to adapt the lesson, responding to what you see and hear. Your aim is to simultaneously keep as many students at the point of 'desirable difficulty', where their work is challenging but achievable.

Dylan Wiliam

EXAMPLE OF A REALLY BIG MISTAKE: CALLING FORMATIVE ASSESSMENT FORMATIVE ASSESSMENT RATHER THAN SOMETHING LIKE 'RESPONSIVE TEACHING'.
(WILIAM, 2013)

Previously, as teachers we discussed differentiation and assessment of learning to secure progress

Despite good intentions, differentiation led to teachers spending hours creating different resources for different students, prejudging their 'ability' before the lesson. For many, this placed a 'glass ceiling' on their attainment, where *some* received a different curriculum from *most*. Likewise, assessment for/of learning started as a sound pedagogical concept related to checking students' understanding, but regrettably became more about tracking data and endless marking of students' work to ensure teachers were accountable for students' progress. Adaptive, responsive teaching is an attempt to move away from this.

1 → 2 → 3 → 4 → 5 → 6

CHAPTER
PROFESSIONAL DEVELOPMENT

52 INTERVIEWS | 53 PERSONAL STATEMENTS | **54 PROFESSIONAL LEARNING** | 55 TEACHER INSIGHTS | 56 THE ECF |
57 THE ECF PT2 | 58 MENTOR MEETINGS | 59 ENGAGING WITH RESEARCH | 60 GLOWING UP, NOT BURNING OUT |
61 TEACHER STUDY PT1 | 62 TEACHER STUDY PT2 | 63 TEACHER STUDY PT3 | 64 TEACHER STUDY PT4 |

Here are some steps to get you started:

To be responsive and adaptive you need to know your students and subject well

Start with useful information: the common misconceptions of the topic; how students make sense of your subject; the particular learning needs of students; absences and relevant information on students' prior attainment. **Tip:** capture this somewhere. I noted it on my seating plans which I used as a live tracker that I updated in lesson with my thoughts.

When planning, consider what your curriculum already has to offer that can support with meaning-making and misconceptions

Word banks, knowledge organisers, models, timelines, diagrams (etc.) are all useful when students get stuck. **Tip:** design support resources for the unit or topic rather than for each lesson and have them to hand if, and only if, you decide the students need them.

Doug Lemov

[HUNTING] DESCRIBES AN IMPORTANT SHIFT: FROM HOPING FOR USEFUL ANSWERS IN-THE-MOMENT TO SEEKING THEM OUT BEFOREHAND. (LEMOV, 2015a)

In lesson, hunt, don't fish

Go hunt for misconceptions by live marking their work, questioning and listening to them. Use what you find to adapt your lesson to address any issues. **Tip:** if you see the same mistake three times, stop the class and address it for everyone.

ITT Core Content Framework

ADAPTING TEACHING IN A RESPONSIVE WAY, INCLUDING BY PROVIDING TARGETED SUPPORT TO PUPILS WHO ARE STRUGGLING, IS LIKELY TO INCREASE PUPIL SUCCESS. (DfE, 2019b)

In lesson, create the feedback loop

Deliberately plan for students to practise what you've taught them. Assess their responses, give them immediate feedback and adapt your teaching, responding to gaps or needs. **Tip:** remember, you're the support: a live model, a reminder, some encouragement or a different example or explanation goes a long way.

As we have seen, all the concepts of teaching have origins, and understanding them can help you develop your practice and shape your teacher judgement.

SPREAD

55

TEACHER INSIGHTS

Seeing teachers in action will support your own
implementation of routines and pedagogical strategies.

The first few weeks

When beginning your first school placement, you will
not teach straight away. You will probably be excited and
nervous about taking your first lesson. Do not worry; it
is natural to feel this way. Use the first few weeks of your
placement to learn the school's systems and routines. These
few weeks are important to help you settle into taking your
first lesson.

Doug Lemov

*DESIGN AND ESTABLISH
AN EFFICIENT ROUTINE
FOR STUDENTS TO ENTER
THE CLASSROOM AND
BEGIN CLASS.
(LEMOV, 2021)*

In most cases, you will get time to observe colleagues
before you start to take your own lessons. This will give
you valuable information about how teachers apply the
systems and build routines with their students. Alongside
this, it gives you a great opportunity to see how established
teachers use the different pedagogy strategies you have been
introduced to at the beginning of your teacher training
course. There is no substitute for seeing teachers in action.

Observing teachers

Many placement schools will provide you with an
observation timetable that gives you the opportunity
to see teachers in the school across a range of subjects.
Although, a large proportion of the observation time will
likely be dedicated to seeing colleagues within your subject
discipline. When observing colleagues, reflect on how they
do the following:

- Start their lesson.

- Explain new content.

- Model new ideas to students before practice.

- Reinforce expectations in their classroom.

- Ask questions.

- Give feedback – written or verbal.

- Give praise.

- End their lesson.

CHAPTER
PROFESSIONAL DEVELOPMENT

52 INTERVIEWS | 53 PERSONAL STATEMENTS | 54 PROFESSIONAL LEARNING | **55 TEACHER INSIGHTS** | 56 THE ECF |
57 THE ECF PT2 | 58 MENTOR MEETINGS | 59 ENGAGING WITH RESEARCH | 60 GLOWING UP, NOT BURNING OUT |
61 TEACHER STUDY PT1 | 62 TEACHER STUDY PT2 | 63 TEACHER STUDY PT3 | 64 TEACHER STUDY PT4 |

When observing these different elements, write down what the teacher does. Try to write down what they say so you can refer back to it at a later stage. This will help you build ideas for how teachers implement the pedagogical principles in the school. An example might be writing down how the teacher gets everyone's attention when moving between a structured task to a teacher's explanation. Or, you might observe a teacher during a structured discussion through questioning. Observe how the teacher asks specific question types during this discussion. Find time at the end to talk to the teacher to ask them about the approach and strategies they used in their lesson.

Observing students

Seeing how students across the age range interact with their teachers and peers in their lessons is extremely beneficial. Find time to talk to the students to ask them about their lessons, the work they have completed in their books, and their own strengths and areas for development within the subject.

Field notes

Before you start teaching your first few lessons, gather information about the students from the teacher of the class you will be teaching. Use a seating plan and annotate it with key information about the students. The insights from the class teacher are valuable to support you with your first few lessons.

SEE **SPREAD 07**
EXAMPLES OF SEATING
PLAN CONSIDERATIONS
AND KEY STUDENT
INFORMATION.

SPREAD

56

THE EARLY CAREER FRAMEWORK
You are entitled to high-quality induction, training and support in your first two years of teaching.

Emma Turner
Research and CPD lead

What is the Early Career Framework? (ECF)
All teachers entering the profession are now entitled to two years' worth of induction, support, mentoring, and access to high-quality CPD from a registered provider. This is a new national entitlement, statutory since September 2021.

Why do we need an Early Career Framework?
In high-performing education systems in other countries, teacher training is usually much longer than in England. The DfE's Carter Review 2015 found that initial teacher education is not long enough and that it is not sufficiently joined up to a programme of development and support for colleagues after they have completed ITE.

Another DfE review in 2019 focusing on recruitment and retention also recognised the pressures that often led to teachers early in their careers leaving the profession.

Who should access the ECF?
The ECF is a reform for schools in England which provides mandatory two year training for all teacher entering the profession as part of their induction phase to become fully qualified against the Teachers' Standards (DfE, 2021).

Tanya Ovenden-Hope

THE ECF SETS OUT WHAT THE GOVERNMENT IN ENGLAND BELIEVES ALL NEW TEACHERS NEED TO KNOW AND SHOULD BE ABLE TO DO AS THEY BEGIN THEIR CAREERS.

When will I do my training?
Every new teacher in their first year is entitled to 10% additional time off timetable to access early career support. This is in addition to statutory PPA time that all teachers receive. In your second year of teaching, this additional time will be 5% off timetable. If you work less than full time, you will need to liaise with your training provider and your headteacher to create a bespoke timetable linked directly to your contract of employment.

1 → 2 → 3 → 4 → 5 → 6

CHAPTER
PROFESSIONAL DEVELOPMENT

52 INTERVIEWS | 53 PERSONAL STATEMENTS | 54 PROFESSIONAL LEARNING | 55 TEACHER INSIGHTS | **56 THE ECF** |
57 THE ECF PT2 | 58 MENTOR MEETINGS | 59 ENGAGING WITH RESEARCH | 60 GLOWING UP, NOT BURNING OUT |
61 TEACHER STUDY PT1 | 62 TEACHER STUDY PT2 | 63 TEACHER STUDY PT3 | 64 TEACHER STUDY PT4 |

What will the structure of the training be?

This will depend on your training provider but is usually made up of a blend of face-to-face events with other local ECTs; online weekly self-study; weekly mentor meetings; and some online group events. Often, your training provider will tailor these to your phase or local group of schools.

Can I fail the ECF?

No. You cannot fail the ECF as it is an entitlement to training and is not assessed. However, your school will work with an 'appropriate body' – an organisation to whom they will submit termly reports (progress reviews) about your progress and development. It is these progress reports that reflect the standard of your practice. The contents of these should never be a surprise, as you should be aware of your development points through your weekly meetings with your mentor and through feedback from your induction tutor. Your progress reports are ideally not written by your mentor but are written by a senior colleague in school. However, in small schools, this may be the same person.

The appropriate body will also check you are receiving your entitlement to time off timetable and that you are being enabled to access ECF training and development.

What is the role of my mentor?

Your mentor is there to help provide professional development and support within school and to meet weekly with you to support your learning within the ECF. They will have received training and support in mentoring and should help to contextualise and develop the learning from the ECF.

Professor Rachel Lofthouse

NEW TEACHERS MOST BENEFIT FROM BEING OFFERED SPACE TO GROW, REFLECT, CONTINUE TO OBSERVE OTHERS AND TO WORK COLLABORATIVELY WITH COLLEAGUES. MENTORING IS AT ITS MOST POWERFUL WHEN IT IS BUILT ON POSITIVE PERSONAL RELATIONSHIPS BETWEEN NOVICE TEACHERS AND THOSE WITH MORE EXPERIENCE.

SPREAD

57

THE EARLY CAREER FRAMEWORK PT2

Emma Turner explains the structure of the ECF, how to manage your ECF workload and how to evidence your engagement.

Emma Turner
Research and CPD lead

THE EARLY CAREER FRAMEWORK CAN BE FOUND IN THE **APPENDIX** OF THIS BOOK.

Reuben Moore

TEACHING IS A TEAM SPORT AND THEREFORE NEW COLLEAGUES SHOULD HAVE THE SUPPORT OF MENTORS AND OTHERS IN SCHOOL AND BEYOND TO HELP.

'During induction, it is essential that early career teachers are able to develop the knowledge, practices and working habits that set them up for a fulfilling and successful career in teaching.' (ECF, 2019)

The eight standards

Within the Early Career Framework there are eight standards.

1. Set high expectations

2. Promote good progress

3. Demonstrate good subject and curriculum knowledge

4. Plan and teach well structured lessons

5. Adapt teaching

6. Make accurate and productive use of assessment

7. Manage behaviour effectively

8. Fulfil wider professional responsibilities

Within each of these eight standards there are 'Learn that' and 'Learn how to' sections. 'Learn that' outlines the knowledge teachers should develop within each standard. 'Learn how to' outlines the practices teachers should learn how to develop in order to then employ judiciously in their day-to-day work. Each of the eight standards also has a referenced research base at the back of each section for further study.

The ECF study blocks

When accessing the ECF provider sessions and the online self-study, each session or block will focus on content from one or more of the eight standards. Although the standards will be addressed in a particular order by your provider, it is important that your mentor and induction tutor also provide timely access to support in the standards that most meet your own specific needs. If, within your practice, you need to focus more or less on a specific aspect of a standard, your mentor can adapt their support to best meet your

CHAPTER
PROFESSIONAL DEVELOPMENT

52 INTERVIEWS | 53 PERSONAL STATEMENTS | 54 PROFESSIONAL LEARNING | 55 TEACHER INSIGHTS | 56 THE ECF |
57 THE ECF PT2 | 58 MENTOR MEETINGS | 59 ENGAGING WITH RESEARCH | 60 GLOWING UP, NOT BURNING OUT |
61 TEACHER STUDY PT1 | 62 TEACHER STUDY PT2 | 63 TEACHER STUDY PT3 | 64 TEACHER STUDY PT4 |

needs. The blocks are designed to be supportive and helpful, not onerous, repeating previously secured content or conflicting with your context and professional needs. Your mentor should help you prioritise your areas of learning and highlight which blocks need further, deeper study or a lighter touch.

Managing your ECF workload

The ECF has been written to support all teachers in all phases. As such, it covers lots of content, some that may not have as much relevance or resonance with your specific phase or subject.

The ECF is designed to be supportive and to provide high-quality support and training. It is not designed to add unnecessarily to teachers' workloads. Many providers recognise that not all content in blocks will be relevant to all teachers in all settings and so 100% completion of training blocks is often not necessary. A recommended percentage engagement or coverage for each block will be available from your provider. Mentors, who have an expert overview of your practice, can then work with you to identify which aspects of the training will be most useful to you and your context. If you are finding it difficult to manage your ECF workload, speak to your mentor or your provider at the earliest opportunity; do not leave it until you feel overwhelmed.

Your weekly meetings with your mentor should include discussion of your learning from the ECF block and these are an ideal time to work together to plan which elements of each block will be most useful to you.

Evidencing your ECF engagement

Most providers' online platforms track your engagement as a percentage online. It is worth noting that any notes or work you do on these platforms is for your own reference; it is not assessed or a two-way platform. Care needs to be taken then not to duplicate work by keeping development notes on multiple platforms.

Early Career Framework, DfE

⟐

HOWEVER, TOO OFTEN, NEW TEACHERS HAVE NOT ENJOYED THE SUPPORT THEY NEED TO THRIVE, NOR HAVE THEY HAD ADEQUATE TIME TO DEVOTE TO THEIR PROFESSIONAL DEVELOPMENT. (DfE, 2019a)

SPREAD

58

MENTOR MEETINGS
Dedicated time to engage in a professional discussion
contributes towards becoming a more reflective practitioner.

The first few weeks

At the beginning of each school placement, you will be assigned a school mentor who will work closely with you throughout your placement. The mentor is usually someone who will work in the same department.

During this first year, you will have regular contact with a school mentor across your different placements. The relationship between you and your mentor will be important in supporting your development. But, what do we mean by mentoring?

Mentoring is defined by the Centre for Use of Research in Evidence and Education (CUREE) as 'a structured, sustained process for supporting professional learners through significant career transitions'.

Professor Rachel Lofthouse

Therefore, your mentor will support you through the different stages of your training from understanding aspects of teaching such as the curriculum, planning your lessons, designing activities, presenting new content to students, and establishing your own classroom expectations.

MENTORING IS AT ITS MOST POWERFUL WHEN IT IS BUILT ON POSITIVE PERSONAL RELATIONSHIPS.

The duration and frequency of your mentor meetings will vary depending on the placement school and the expectations outlined by your ITT provider. Familiarise yourself with the guidance before starting your school placement. Once you know who your mentor will be at your placement school, send them an introductory email with key information about yourself that you would like them to know. Alongside your introduction, ask your mentor a few key questions that can help you prepare for the first few days and weeks. This might include asking for an example of the curriculum and typical lessons that are taught. Also, research the school by looking at key information on the website, including behaviour and teaching and learning policies.

CHAPTER
PROFESSIONAL DEVELOPMENT

52 INTERVIEWS | 53 PERSONAL STATEMENTS | 54 PROFESSIONAL LEARNING | 55 TEACHER INSIGHTS | 56 THE ECF |
57 THE ECF PT2 | **58 MENTOR MEETINGS** | 59 ENGAGING WITH RESEARCH | 60 GLOWING UP, NOT BURNING OUT |
61 TEACHER STUDY PT1 | 62 TEACHER STUDY PT2 | 63 TEACHER STUDY PT3 | 64 TEACHER STUDY PT4 |

What should you expect from your mentor?

Every mentor will be different, which will mean you will
need to adapt. However, you should expect that your
mentor will:

- Be approachable and accessible.

- Listen attentively.

- Provide concrete examples to support your development.

- Create opportunities for you to develop and learn new
  pedagogy strategies.

- Be passionate, positive and professional acting as a role
  model.

- Encourage you to make decisions.

- Encourage you to try new strategies.

Haili Hughes

*HAVING SUPPORTIVE
MENTORS AND
EXPERIENCED
COLLEAGUES TO SUPPORT
CAN MAKE A HUGE
DIFFERENCE.*

What will your mentor expect from you?

Before starting your mentor meetings, it is useful to know
some of the etiquettes.

Honesty – As you develop a professional relationship with
your mentor, be open and honest about aspects of your
training year and the school that you find challenging. The
mentor is there to support you, but unless they know the
things you struggle with, they won't be able to help.

Organisation – Your mentor may have an agenda that
they will want to cover for each of your meetings. Try to
plan ahead and consider the key points that you will be
discussing in the meeting beforehand.

Open and reflective – There will be times when you plan a
lesson and it doesn't quite go as you would like. While it can
be frustrating, this is normal; even experienced teachers
encounter this. What's important is acknowledging this
and reflecting on what you could do differently next time.

SPREAD

59

ENGAGING WITH RESEARCH

Kate Jones shares her top tips for becoming an evidence-informed and reflective practitioner.

Kate Jones
Senior associate for teaching and learning with evidence-based education

Why lifelong professional learning and development matter

Being an evidence-informed and reflective teacher is to be a teacher that is committed to self-improvement and development. Schools are the embodiment of learning and this doesn't just apply to the students, but all teachers and leaders at all levels. Embracing professional learning early in your career will give you greater understanding, knowledge, resilience and confidence. It is important to show an awareness of strengths and areas that can be further improved.

Professional learning can be low-cost with a high impact

Be willing and open to invite colleagues to watch you teach and be receptive to their feedback. Ask colleagues if you can watch them teach and if possible visit a local school and observe teachers there too. Another option is to record yourself teaching and watch it back, listening to your explanations, questions and interactions with students.

Dylan Wiliam

EVERY TEACHER NEEDS TO IMPROVE, NOT BECAUSE THEY ARE NOT GOOD ENOUGH, BUT BECAUSE THEY CAN BE EVEN BETTER.
(WILIAM, 2016)

There is a wide range of books online but it can be difficult to find time to read as much as we would like. Make it a habit to regularly read articles and blogs. Subscriptions are often free, or low-cost, and can help you stay informed with the latest developments in education as well as offering advice and guidance, and sharing the latest findings from research. In terms of research, seek out research summaries over journals, as they contain the core content without the jargon and can be read much quicker and with greater ease.

Find and join a PLC – professional learning community

Teaching can be lonely and challenging at times. This is why it is so important to find and be part of a professional learning community (PLC). A PLC can offer guidance, support, encouragement and friendship. A PLC is a group of educators that collaborate or network. An example of this can be a subject association or a group of educators

CHAPTER
PROFESSIONAL DEVELOPMENT

52 INTERVIEWS | 53 PERSONAL STATEMENTS | 54 PROFESSIONAL LEARNING | 55 TEACHER INSIGHTS | 56 THE ECF |
57 THE ECF PT2 | 58 MENTOR MEETINGS | **59 ENGAGING WITH RESEARCH** | 60 GLOWING UP, NOT BURNING OUT |
61 TEACHER STUDY PT1 | 62 TEACHER STUDY PT2 | 63 TEACHER STUDY PT3 | 64 TEACHER STUDY PT4 |

with a shared interest or in the same local area. A PLC is a place to learn, share and grow with other professionals in education.

Be selective and be careful with your time

There is a vast amount of professional learning content and opportunities but the quality does vary considerably. The sheer amount available can be overwhelming and intimidating. It can feel challenging to try to keep up with emerging trends, developments and reading all the latest blogs or books because, quite simply, we can't and shouldn't strive to do so. Think carefully about how your time, effort and energy is spent trying to improve and develop.

We believe all great teachers have one key element in common; they never stop learning. We also believe that all great schools have one thing in common; they never stop improving. A great teacher will flourish at a school that encourages them to keep learning. A great school will only be able to improve with teachers that never stop learning. Teacher development and school improvement go hand in hand.

Kate Jones and Robin Macpherson, The Teaching Life (2021)

GLOWING UP, NOT BURNING OUT

In the midst of caring for your students, don't forget to care for yourself.

Dr Poppy Gibson
Senior lecturer and course lead in primary education

Professor Michael Green
Associate executive director of strategic development and visiting professor

Self-care isn't selfish

Teaching is a job where we are continually putting others first; how can we meet the needs of our students? How can we adapt our teaching to facilitate learning? What resources do we need to prepare? It is essential in a job as altruistic as ours to remember that self-care is not selfish, and in fact it is quite the opposite; it is selfless and essential for you to be feeling well in order to be the best teacher you can be for your students.

'Burnout' is when we are in a state of being both physically and mentally exhausted; by building self-care into our daily schedules, we can help avoid it.

Self-care strategies?

Here are some simple self-care strategies that can fit around a teacher's lifestyle:

- Have a box full of healthy snacks, such as cereal bars or protein balls, stored in your room. On those days you are too busy for a proper lunch, you can ensure you have a quick pick-me-up at hand.

- Leave everything ready on a Friday. Set up your Monday visual timetable, books, worksheets etc., so that Monday morning is as stress-free as possible.

- Download a mindfulness app or keep a journal to allow space for daily reflection.

- Put up a board showing your weekly meal planner – fuelling your stomach well will help fuel your mind.

- Take up a new hobby, such as gardening, golf, baking or paint by numbers. Keep your students updated on your progress; this also allows you to prioritise time for you while building new skills.

Establish a life beyond school; developing work parameters

Teaching is a job that can become mentally consuming – could you save that yoghurt pot for an art lesson?

CHAPTER
PROFESSIONAL DEVELOPMENT

52 INTERVIEWS | 53 PERSONAL STATEMENTS | 54 PROFESSIONAL LEARNING | 55 TEACHER INSIGHTS | 56 THE ECF | 57 THE ECF PT2 | 58 MENTOR MEETINGS | 59 ENGAGING WITH RESEARCH | **60 GLOWING UP, NOT BURNING OUT** | 61 TEACHER STUDY PT1 | 62 TEACHER STUDY PT2 | 63 TEACHER STUDY PT3 | 64 TEACHER STUDY PT4 |

Whiteboard pens on sale in the supermarket. Wondering about a child's behaviour that day that was out of character. With a profession that involves so much emotion and energy, it is essential you try to establish a life beyond school in order to promote a healthy work–life balance. Although 'switching off' is sometimes easier said than done, manage this by not checking or sending emails after a certain time, making networks with people other than just teachers to vary discussion, or plan for a 'switch-off Sunday' – no work, no planning, and aim to visit somewhere new or spend time outside or with someone to provide a full break from work.

Prioritise

Stephen Covey created a time-management matrix that helps us to categorise the tasks we need to do by their importance and urgency. To help prioritise things you need to do, consider using the four quadrants and writing each of the tasks into the appropriate box. There are only 24 hours in the day, and it is likely some things will need to wait until tomorrow; you are only human, after all. Using Covey's matrix helps you to reflect upon the urgency and importance of tasks to be able to work through them in an order that leads to better management of workload, and ultimately more job satisfaction.

To avoid burnout, don't forget to add some self-care tasks to that quadrant too; how about cook your favourite meal, take a walk, or spend an hour on the hobby you recently started?

SPREAD

61

TEACHER STUDY PT1

Keavy Lowden reflects on classroom systems and routines in Year One of her teaching.

Keavy Lowden
English teacher

Strong start

Welcoming your students into the classroom while standing at the door allows for optimum control over the way students enter the room. Correcting loud, lively behaviour outside results in a calm presence when moving into the classroom, reducing any potential low-level disruption or behaviour when starting the lesson. Greeting at the door also allows for individual check-ins, which help build positive student–teacher relationships and thus mutual respect.

Building relationships

While building relationships with students is important, ensuring you build bonds with colleagues is also crucial. Professional relationships allow you to become the best teacher possible, through sharing and implementing different teaching methods, materials and pedagogy observed and shared with others. Finally, building relationships with students' parents/carers is the ultimate completion of gaining trust and respect from parents, who expect their children to be receiving optimum learning. It also helps strengthen the relationship built with each student, by informing parents/carers of their child's progress, praise, and areas for improvement.

Barak Rosenshine

ASK A LARGE NUMBER OF QUESTIONS AND CHECK THE RESPONSES OF ALL STUDENTS.

Routines

Establishing routines ties in with setting high expectations; both depend on each other to work. Establishing routines from the initial offset should allow for students to be clear on the expectations and consequences of these being flouted. High expectations create non-biased and fair environments, with equality for all. For example, setting the expectation that everyone will provide an answer for the starter questions and using their whiteboard to share with the whole class shows you care about all students' learning.

CHAPTER
PROFESSIONAL DEVELOPMENT

52 INTERVIEWS | 53 PERSONAL STATEMENTS | 54 PROFESSIONAL LEARNING | 55 TEACHER INSIGHTS | 56 THE ECF |
57 THE ECF PT2 | 58 MENTOR MEETINGS | 59 ENGAGING WITH RESEARCH | 60 GLOWING UP, NOT BURNING OUT |
61 TEACHER STUDY PT1 | 62 TEACHER STUDY PT2 | 63 TEACHER STUDY PT3 | 64 TEACHER STUDY PT4 |

High expectations

Setting high expectations is necessary to set boundaries and create the mutual respect expected of all students and staff within a school. Establishing and setting high expectations – typically in line with the school's policy on high expectations and behaviour – allows everybody in the school to behave and conduct themselves in a universal manner that is easy to remember and leads to equality and respect.

Seating plans

Seating plans can aid and support the learning of all students within the classroom, especially when using Cold Call. Having a hard copy of a seating plan allows the teacher to randomly call on any student to provide an answer or an idea. This allows the teacher to gain clear insight into all students' comprehension of the given topic, regardless of ability and gender.

A seating plan ensures that order and structure are established in the classroom before learning takes place. It allows students to recognise that the teacher has possession and control of the situation, which helps form mutual respect.

A seating plan helps massively with the support provided by the teacher or teaching assistants to students. Strategically placing students who need additional learning support in a suitable place within the class (typically nearer to the front of the room) allows for an opportunity for support and therefore learning.

SPREAD

62

TEACHER STUDY PT2

Clarry Simpson offers her insights on how to get it right in Year One.

Clarry Simpson
ECT induction lead
and geography
teacher

Why is subject knowledge so important?

The fourth and eighth blocks of the Early Career Framework encourage early career teachers to develop their knowledge of their subjects.

If you have a sound understanding of the knowledge you are teaching, you can meet the teaching standards on progress, structured lessons, adaptive teaching and assessment in meaningful ways.

I firmly believe that our learners deserve to be faced with experts in the subjects that they are offered in school – teachers who are passionate and ignite a passion in those in their classroom.

If you are reading this, you probably have a degree in a relevant subject that relates to your teaching topic, you have a love of learning and an enthusiasm for the subject you have chosen to share with the next generation of students – you know the power of knowledge.

In Daniel Willingham's book *Why Don't Students Like School?* he proposes that knowledge is the key foundation in which the brain can then develop skills. The knowledge comes first. Willingham gives powerful examples of where teachers use analogies in their practice to make concepts hold in students' long-term memory – only a teacher with a secure subject knowledge base can do this.

Early career teachers should utilise their fantastic community networks, which can help support subject knowledge.

How can you develop your subject knowledge?

Using subject associations, experienced staff, multi-academy trust meetings, local networks such as TeachMeets, researchED, the wider teaching community (e.g. on Twitter) and university alumni groups, can help to develop a core understanding of the subject matter that they are teaching. If a teacher can show their students a

CHAPTER
PROFESSIONAL DEVELOPMENT

52 INTERVIEWS | 53 PERSONAL STATEMENTS | 54 PROFESSIONAL LEARNING | 55 TEACHER INSIGHTS | 56 THE ECF |
57 THE ECF PT2 | 58 MENTOR MEETINGS | 59 ENGAGING WITH RESEARCH | 60 GLOWING UP, NOT BURNING OUT |
61 TEACHER STUDY PT1 | **62 TEACHER STUDY PT2** | 63 TEACHER STUDY PT3 | 64 TEACHER STUDY PT4 |

love of learning, it will motivate them to be curious learners themselves. Are you setting enough time aside for subject-related study?

What does this look like?

When observing a successful early career teacher, I love to hear phrases like 'I was reading this book that told me that… I was listening to a podcast called x that explained the Cold War as… So many non-scientists think [this misconception] but we know that this isn't right, don't we?'

I hear students passionately telling their teacher about a documentary that they saw relating to the subject or how they corrected a friend or parent on their understanding of something the student themselves had learned in class the previous week.

Questions to ask yourself

Start with the topics you are going to be teaching:

- What are the key concepts that help the learning stick? What concepts are you linking this to?

- What questions do you have about the knowledge/ concept?

- What questions do you expect the learners to have about the knowledge/concept?

- What are the likely misconceptions?

- How are you going to present the material so that it links to what students already know and expand this knowledge further? What analogies are you going to use?

- How will you check understanding?

SPREAD

63

TEACHER STUDY PT3

The key to securing understanding is to never assume what students already know.

Amy Lyon
History teacher

Checking for understanding at every stage is vital

Never assume that students know anything. Assuming that students know even the simplest of concepts is the easiest way to prevent progression due to lack of understanding and existence of misconceptions. Checking for knowledge and understanding at every stage of the lesson is vital, whether it be everyday concepts or specialist knowledge.

Powerful questioning checks for prior understanding

Questioning should always be underpinned by the principle of never assuming what students know. Ask students what key terms and concepts in your subject mean, but also ensure to check for understanding of everyday words. You will either confirm understanding or be provided with the opportunity to explain and remove misconceptions.

Barak Rosenshine

PROVIDING GUIDED PRACTICE AFTER TEACHING SMALL AMOUNTS OF NEW MATERIAL, AND CHECKING FOR STUDENT UNDERSTANDING, CAN HELP LIMIT THE DEVELOPMENT OF MISCONCEPTIONS.

Questioning should also be used to check for understanding of a task. Never assume that students will know what to do once you have explained the task once. Ask students what the first thing is that they will do when you set them off on a task. What is the next thing they should do when that is finished? Often, you will identify misconceptions or misunderstandings regarding the expectations of the task that can be cleared before students begin their work. However, ensure to direct questions, using Cold Calling, to various students in the class since you cannot assume that there is a class understanding if only a select few students respond to your questions.

Similarly, never assume that students already know how to do a common task, such as a mind map. The simplest of tasks may seem clear, but modelling at least the first question on a worksheet or the first branch of a mind map provides explicit instruction and scaffolding for those who may require further support within the class.

CHAPTER
PROFESSIONAL DEVELOPMENT

52 INTERVIEWS | 53 PERSONAL STATEMENTS | 54 PROFESSIONAL LEARNING | 55 TEACHER INSIGHTS | 56 THE ECF |
57 THE ECF PT2 | 58 MENTOR MEETINGS | 59 ENGAGING WITH RESEARCH | 60 GLOWING UP, NOT BURNING OUT |
61 TEACHER STUDY PT1 | 62 TEACHER STUDY PT2 | **63 TEACHER STUDY PT3** | 64 TEACHER STUDY PT4 |

Never assume that knowledge has moved into the long-term memory

It is easy to assume that students have moved knowledge into the long-term memory after covering content thoroughly and embedding it into retrieval. However, you should never assume that it will remain in the long term memory. Even concepts that are used in each lesson and seem somewhat simple in comparison to more difficult concepts should be covered in retrieval practice throughout the curriculum. This is to ensure understanding of the concept remains within the long-term memory as you move forward. Often the simpler concepts underpin the more complex, thus proving understanding and recall of them to be vital to make progression.

Introduce students to revision methods, no matter how simple

When asking students to revise, never assume that they have a bank of revision methods to their knowledge. Introduce students to revision methods, even those as simple as flashcards and mind maps. Often we assume that students simply know how to revise when we ask them to, but many find the task of how to revise more challenging than revisiting subject content.

SPREAD

64

TEACHER STUDY PT4

Shannon McCarthy reflects on fulfilling the wider
responsibilities of a teacher in Year One of her teaching.

Shannon McCarthy
Art teacher

Wider responsibilities

During my PGCE, I found my placements to be a lot more
impactful to my training than university lead lectures,
assignments, and enrichment activities. With this in mind,
pastoral is one of the areas where school-based experience
played such a strong role in understanding the correct
ways to react to a situation then and there, in the moment,
concerning both student and parent.

In my training, I have had opportunities to gain experience
with leading parents' evening (both online and in-person),
observing and taking part within a form group, emailing
parents home, delivering PSHE lessons and reporting
safeguarding of students in need. I found that having
discussions with my mentor about the situations was very
important in how to approach particular conversations
in the utmost professional manner, which comes from
experience. An example of this was when a student
confided in me a worry of beginning an eating disorder
and harming themselves. This, of course, is a very delicate
situation and had to be addressed most correctly, from
reporting to the safeguarding lead to the type of dialogue
that is used towards the student.

There are so many different types of safeguarding
issues that may arise in my teaching career but from the
experiences that I've encountered so far, I've learned that
it is always best to discuss it with the appropriate person,
especially those who are trained within that area, to
learn more about specific situations and become more
knowledgeable in how to address these issues in the future.

Parents' evening

Another experience that I see as a critical learning point
was my involvement in parents' evenings. During my first
placement, some things were still impacted by COVID-19
and parents' evening was one of them. Due to this, the
session was delivered online, and parents were able to use

CHAPTER
PROFESSIONAL DEVELOPMENT

52 INTERVIEWS | 53 PERSONAL STATEMENTS | 54 PROFESSIONAL LEARNING | 55 TEACHER INSIGHTS | 56 THE ECF |
57 THE ECF PT2 | 58 MENTOR MEETINGS | 59 ENGAGING WITH RESEARCH | 60 GLOWING UP, NOT BURNING OUT |
61 TEACHER STUDY PT1 | 62 TEACHER STUDY PT2 | 63 TEACHER STUDY PT3 | **64 TEACHER STUDY PT4**

the software to book slots with teachers in four-minute increments. I undertook this parents' evening with two of the Year 8 art classes I taught and found myself to be booked up for the night, but only being able to talk to 25 of the 65 students in those two classes. Even though I found the build-up towards my first solo parents' evening very nerve-racking, I found this to be a great experience where I learned so many new things, such as how to address parents and discuss any student issues in the classroom, and – of course – it was a great confidence booster too! My favourite thing about parents' evening was giving praise about the students to both themselves and their parents and seeing their smiles – it felt so rewarding!

PSHE

A pastoral experience that I undertook (that took me by surprise because of how much I enjoyed delivering it) was teaching PSHE lessons to Year 9. I was quite worried when I was told I would start picking up these lessons, as it isn't art-related and I'm not a 'specialist' within that area. However, I'm more of a 'specialist' than I thought. The first few sessions that I delivered were based on applying for a job, personal statements, and interviews. These were all things that I was exploring myself just a few weeks before applying for and being accepted for my first teaching post.

As it was still in the forefront of my mind, I thought it was important to use my personal experience in the lessons and discuss my recent interview experience and the route I had taken to get to that place. However, there were a lot of students in the class who weren't sure of what they wanted to do for a career, so I also shared my experience of applying to my first Saturday job when I was 15, as it was more relevant to them at that moment in time, which also helped with student engagement.

REFERENCES

Agarwal, K. P. (2019), WHAT IS RETRIEVAL PRACTICE?, www.retrievalpractice.org/why-it-works

Ashbee, R. (2021), CURRICULUM: THEORY, CULTURE AND THE SUBJECT SPECIALISMS, Routledge, Abingdon, UK

Ball, D. L. (1990), THE MATHEMATICAL UNDERSTANDINGS THAT PROSPECTIVE TEACHERS BRING TO TEACHER EDUCATION, The Elementary School Journal, (90)4: 449–466

Beale, S. (2021), HISTORY HOW TO'S: FOLDING FRENZY, https://mrthorntonteach.files.wordpress.com/2021/03/how-to-folding-frenzy.pdf

Bennett, T. (2020a), RUNNING THE ROOM, John Catt Ltd, Woodbridge, UK

Bennett, T. (2020b), USE MORE PRAISE THAN PUNISHMENT, www.tes.com/magazine/archive/use-more-praise-punishment-study-tells-teachers

Berger, R. (2003), AN ETHIC OF EXCELLENCE: BUILDING A CULTURE OF CRAFTSMANSHIP WITH STUDENTS, Heinemann Educational Books, New Hampshire, US

Boxer, A. (2022), TO MAKE SURE YOU STUDENTS ARE READY TO PRACTISE, USE MINI-WHITEBOARDS, https://tipsforteachers.co.uk/adam-boxer/

Boxer, A. (2020), FRONT-LOADING, https://achemicalorthodoxy.wordpress.com/2020/10/14/front-loading/

British Dyslexia Association. (2018), CREATING A DYSLEXIA FRIENDLY WORKPLACE, www.bdadyslexia.org.uk/advice/employers/creating-a-dyslexia-friendly-workplace/dyslexia-friendly-style-guide#:~:text=Use%20sans%20serif%20fonts%2C%20such,may%20request%20a%20larger%20font

Cairo, A. (2013), THE FUNCTIONAL ART, New Riders, Berkeley, US

Caviglioli, O. (2019), DUAL CODING WITH TEACHERS, John Catt Ltd, Woodbridge, UK

Centre for Use of Research in Evidence and Education (CUREE). (2005), MENTORING AND COACHING CPD CAPACITY BUILDING PROJECT: NATIONAL FRAMEWORK FOR MENTORING AND COACHING, www.curee.co.uk/files/publication/1219925968/National-framework-for-mentoring-and-coaching.pdf

Chiles, M. (2020), THE CRAFT OF ASSESSMENT, John Catt Ltd, Woodbridge, UK

Chiles, M. (2021), THE SWEET SPOT, John Catt Ltd, Woodbridge, UK

Chiles, M. (2021), THE FEEDBACK PENDULUM, John Catt Ltd, Woodbridge, UK

Clark, R. C. & Mayer, R. E. (2016), E-LEARNING AND SCIENCE INSTRUCTION, Wiley, New Jersey

DfE. (2015), CARTER REVIEW OF INITIAL TEACHER TRAINING, DfE, London

DfE. (2019a), EARLY CAREER FRAMEWORK, DfE, London

DfE. (2019b), ITT CORE CONTENT FRAMEWORK, DfE, London, licensed under the Open Government Licence, https://assets.publishing.service.gov.uk/government/uploads/system/uploads/attachment_data/file/974307/ITT_core_content_framework_.pdf

DfE. (2019c), TEACHER RECRUITMENT AND RETENTION STRATEGY, DfE, London

DfE. (2021), TEACHERS' STANDARDS, DfE, London

Didau, D. (2018a), IT'S ALL ABOUT RELATIONSHIPS, https://learningspy.co.uk/behaviour/its-all-about-relationships/

Didau, D. (2018b), HOW TO EXPLAIN…SCHEMA, https://learningspy.co.uk/featured/how-to-explain-schema/

Kaiser, N. (2020), MEANINGFUL MEMORY, https://researchschool.org.uk/norwich/news/meaningful-memory

Dunlosky, J. (2013), STRENGTHENING THE STUDENT TOOLBOX, American Educator

Education Endowment Foundation. (2017), IMPROVING MATHEMATICS IN KEY STAGES 2 AND 3, https://educationendowmentfoundation.org.uk/education-evidence/guidance-reports/maths-ks-2-3

Education Endowment Foundation. (2018a), MAKING BEST USE OF TEACHING ASSISTANTS GUIDANCE REPORT, https://d2tic4wvo1iusb.cloudfront.net/eef-guidance-reports/teaching-assistants/TA_Guidance_Report_MakingBestUseOfTeachingAssistants-Printable_2021-11-02-162019_wsqd.pdf?v=1635870019

Education Endowment Foundation. (2018b), METACOGNITION AND SELF-REGULATED LEARNING, SEVEN RECOMMENDATIONS FOR TEACHING SELF-REGULATED LEARNING & METACOGNITION, https://educationendowmentfoundation.org.uk/education-evidence/guidance-reports/metacognition

Education Endowment Foundation. (2018c), IMPROVING LITERACY IN SECONDARY SCHOOLS GUIDANCE REPORT, https://educationendowmentfoundation.org.uk/education-evidence/guidance-reports/literacy-ks3-ks4

Education Endowment Foundation. (2021), HOMEWORK, https://educationendowmentfoundation.org.uk/education-evidence/teaching-learning-toolkit/homework

Fernández-Alonso, R., Suárez-Álvarez, J. & Muñiz, J. (2015), ADOLESCENTS' HOMEWORK PERFORMANCE IN MATHEMATICS AND SCIENCE: PERSONAL FACTORS AND TEACHING PRACTICES, Journal of Educational Psychology, 107(4): 1075–1085

Furst, E. (2022), MODELING THE LEARNING PROCESS, https://sites.google.com/view/efratfurst/pyramidmodel

Hammond, Z. (2014), CULTURALLY RESPONSIVE TEACHING AND THE BRAIN: PROMOTING AUTHENTIC ENGAGEMENT AND RIGOR AMONG CULTURALLY AND LINGUISTICALLY DIVERSE STUDENTS, SAGE Publications, California, US

Hattie, J. (2008), VISIBLE LEARNING: A SYNTHESIS OF OVER 800 META-ANALYSES RELATING TO ACHIEVEMENT, Routledge, Abingdon, UK

Hattie, J. (2021), CLOSING THOUGHTS FROM JOHN HATTIE. In Chiles, M., The Feedback Pendulum, John Catt Ltd, Woodbridge, UK

REFERENCES

Hendrick, C. (2022), TWITTER 21.03.22, https://twitter.com/C_Hendrick/status/1505838514352574464?s=20&t=LHwsjvjurbC0dvWHkzSfrQ

Hughes, H. (2021), MENTORING IN SCHOOLS: THE KEY TO RETAINING EARLY CAREER TEACHERS?, https://blog.irisconnect.com/uk/mentoring-in-schools#:~:text=Mentoring%20is%20at%20its%20most%20powerful%20when%20it,Lofthouse%20in%20%E2%80%98Mentoring%20in%20Schools%E2%80%99%20by%20Haili%20Hughes

Jones, K. (2021), HOW TO EMBED RETRIEVAL PRACTICE INTO YOUR SCHOOL'S CURRICULUM, https://blog.innerdrive.co.uk/retrieval-practice-and-curriculum-design

Jones, K. & Macpherson, R. (2021), THE TEACHING LIFE: PROFESSIONAL LEARNING AND CAREER PROGRESSION, John Catt Ltd, Woodbridge, UK

Kara, B. (2021), DIVERSITY: WAYS INTO CURRICULUM BUILDING. In Sherrington, T. and Caviglioli, O., Teaching Walkthrus 2: Five-step Guides to Instructional Coaching (pp. 58-59). John Catt Ltd, Woodbridge, UK

Kirschner, P. A. & Hendrick, C. (2020), HOW LEARNING HAPPENS: SEMINAL WORKS IN EDUCATIONAL PSYCHOLOGY AND WHAT THEY MEAN IN PRACTICE, Routledge, Abingdon, UK

Lemov, D. (2015a), HUNTING VERSUS FISHING, https://teachlikeachampion.com/blog/hunting-versus-fishing/

Lemov, D. (2015b), TEACH LIKE A CHAMPION 2.0, 62 TECHNIQUES THAT PUT STUDENTS ON THE PATH TO COLLEGE, Jossey-Bass, San Francisco, US

Lemov, D. (2021), TEACH LIKE A CHAMPION 3.0: 63 TECHNIQUES THAT PUT STUDENTS N THE PATH TO COLLEGE, Jossey-Bass, San Francisco, US

Lofthouse, R. (2021), MENTORING IN SCHOOLS: THE KEY TO RETAINING EARLY CAREER TEACHERS? https://blog.irisconnect.com/uk/mentoring-in-schools#:~:text=Mentoring%20is%20at%20its%20most%20powerful%20when%20it,Lofthouse%20in%20%E2%80%98Mentoring%20in%20Schools%E2%80%99%20by%20Haili%20Hughes

Marzano, R. J., Pickering, D. J. & Pollock, J. E. (2001), CLASSROOM INSTRUCTION THAT WORKS: RESEARCH-BASED STRATEGIES FIR INCREASING STUDENT ACHIEVEMENT, Pearson, USA.

Mccrea, P. (2017), MEMORABLE TEACHING: LEVERAGING MEMORY TO BUILD DEEP AND DURABLE LEARNING IN THE CLASSROOM: 2 (HIGH IMPACT TEACHING), printed by the author.

Moore, R. (2021), FOREWORD BY REUBEN MOORE. In Hughes, H. (2021), Mentoring in Schools: How to become an expert colleague, Crown House Publishing Ltd, Carmarthen, Wales.

Morgan, J. (2022), MODEL TECHNIQUES LIVE, https://tipsforteachers.co.uk/model-live/

Mulholland, M. (2022), In Thompson, A. and Walsh, K., Teacher Handbook: SEND, licensed under the Open Government Licence.

Murphy, J. & Murphy, D. (2018) THINKING READING: WHAT EVERY SECONDARY TEACHER NEEDS TO KNOW ABOUT READING, John Catt Ltd, Woodbridge, UK

Myatt, M. (2021), ABOVE THEIR PAY GRADE, www.marymyatt.com/blog/above-their-pay-grade?format=amp

Myatt, M. (2022a), HOW RICH VOCABULARY HELPS PUPILS TO LEARN THE CURRICULUM, www.marymyatt.com/blog/how-rich-vocabulary-helps-pupils-to-learn-the-curriculum

Myatt, M. (2022b), HOW HIGH CHALLENGE AND LOW THREAT CAN HELP PUPILS TO LEARN THE CURRICULUM, www.marymyatt.com/blog/how-high-challenge-and-low-threat-can-help-pupils-to-learn-the-curriculum

Ovenden-Hope, T. (2022), THE EARLY CAREER FRAMEWORK: ORIGINS, OUTCOMES AND OPPORTUNITIES, John Catt Ltd, Woodbridge, UK

Pace, D. & Price, M. (2005), INSTRUCTIONAL TECHNIQUES TO FACILITATE INCLUSIVE EDUCATION. In D. Schwartz (ed.), Including Children with Special Needs (pp. 115–131). Westport, CT: Greenwood Press

Pritchard, B. (2022), EEF BLOG: WORKING WITH WORKED EXAMPLES – SIMPLE TECHNIQUES TO ENHANCE THEIR EFFECTIVENESS, https://educationendowmentfoundation.org.uk/news/eef-blog-working-with-worked-examples-simple-techniques-to-enhance-their-effectiveness

Quigley, A. (2013), EXPLANATIONS: TOP 10 TEACHING TIPS, www.theconfidentteacher.com/2013/05/explanations-top-ten-teaching-tips/

Quigley, A. (2020), 6 EXCELLENT ETYMOLOGIES, www.theconfidentteacher.com/2020/06/6-excellent-etymologies/

Quigley, A. (2021), DEVELOPING READING FLUENCY. In Sherrington, T. and Caviglioli, O., Teaching Walkthrus 2: Five-step Guides to Instructional Coaching (pp. 80-81). John Catt Ltd, Woodbridge, UK

Rogers, B. (2007), BEHAVIOUR MANAGEMENT: A WHOLE-SCHOOL APPROACH, Sage Publications, London, UK

Rosenshine, B. (2012), PRINCIPLES OF INSTRUCTION: RESEARCH-BASED STRATEGIES THAT ALL TEACHERS SHOULD KNOW, American Educator

Schacter, D. (2021), THE SEVEN SINS OF MEMORY: HOW THE MIND FORGETS AND REMEMBERS, Houghton Mifflin Boston, MA, US

Sherrington, T. (2017), TEACHING TO THE TOP: ATTITUDES AND STRATEGIES FOR DELIVERING REAL CHALLENGE, https://teacherhead.com/2017/05/28/teaching-to-the-top-attitudes-and-strategies-for-delivering-real-challenge/

Sherrington, T. (2020), THE ART OF MODELLING... IT'S ALL IN THE HANDOVER. https://teacherhead.com/2020/11/28/the-art-of-modelling-its-all-in-the-handover/

Sherrington, T. (2021a), EVERYDAY ROUTINES. CLASSROOM DIALOGUE AND BEHAVIOUR MANAGEMENT, HAND-IN-HAND, https://teacherhead.com/2021/04/12/classroom-dialogue-and-behaviour-management-hand-in-hand/

Sherrington, T. (2021b), CHECK FOR UNDERSTANDING… WHY IT MATTERS AND HOW TO DO IT. #REDSURREY21, https://teacherhead.com/2021/10/17/check-for-understanding-why-it-matters-and-how-to-do-it-redsurrey21/

Sherrington, T. (2022), FIVE WAYS TO: WEAVE READING INTO THE CURRICULUM, https://teacherhead.com/2022/05/05/five-ways-to-weave-reading-into-the-curriculum/

Sherrington, T. & Caviglioli, O. (2020), TEACHING WALKTHRUS, FIVE-STEP GUIDES TO INSTRUCTIONAL COACHING, John Catt Ltd, Woodbridge, UK

Sherrington, T. & Caviglioli, O. (2021), TEACHING WALKTHRUS 2, FIVE-STEP GUIDES TO INSTRUCTIONAL COACHING, John Catt Ltd, Woodbridge, UK

Sherrington, T. & Caviglioli, O. (2022), TEACHING WALKTHRUS 3, FIVE-STEP GUIDES TO INSTRUCTIONAL COACHING, John Catt Ltd, Woodbridge, UK

Spielman, A. (2022), AMANDA SPIELMAN'S SPEECH AT THE 2022 SCHOOLS AND ACADEMIES SHOW, www.gov.uk/government/speeches/amanda-spielmans-speech-at-the-2022-schools-and-academies-show

Strickland, S. (2020), EDUCATION EXPOSED: LEADING A SCHOOL IN A TIME OF UNCERTAINTY, John Catt Ltd, Woodbridge, UK

Sweller, J. (2017), JOHN SWELLER - ACE CONFERENCE/RESEARCHED MELBOURNE, www.youtube.com/watch?v=gOLPfi9Ls-w

Tayler, L. (2021), TWITTER 28.02.21, https://twitter.com/geotayler/status/1365960941830082561

Evidence Based Education. (2020) EXPLAINING: PART OF THE GREAT TEACHING TOOLKIT, https://evidencebased.education/explaining/

Wannarka, R. & Ruhl, K. (2008), SEATING ARRANGEMENTS THAT PROMOTE POSITIVE ACADEMIC AND BEHAVIOURAL OUTCOMES: A REVIEW OF EMPIRICAL RESEARCH, www.corelearn.com/files/Archer/Seating_Arrangements.pdf#:~:text=Seating%20arrangements%20are%20important%20classroom%20settingevents%20because%20they,seated%20in%20rows%2Cwith%20disruptive%20students%20bene%EF%AC%81ting%20the%20most

Webb, J. (2021), THE METACOGNITION HANDBOOK, John Catt Ltd, Woodbridge, UK

Wiliam, D. (2006), INSIDE THE BLACK BOX: RAISING STANDARDS THROUGH CLASSROOM ASSESSMENT, GL Assessment Ltd, London

Wiliam, D. (2013), TWITTER 23.10.13, https://twitter.com/dylanwiliam/status/393045049337847808

Wiliam, D. (2014), IS THE FEEDBACK YOU'RE GIVING STUDENTS HELPING OR HINDERING?, www.dylanwiliamcenter.com/2014/11/29/is-the-feedback-you-are-giving-students-helping-or-hindering/

Wiliam, D. (2016), LEADERSHIP FOR TEACHER LEARNING, Learning Sciences International, USA

Wiliam, D. (2017), TWITTER 26.01.2017, https://twitter.com/dylanwiliam/status/8246825046029434 89?lang=en-GB

Wiliam, D. & Leahy, S. (2015), EMBEDDING FORMATIVE ASSESSMENT: PRACTICAL TECHNIQUES FOR K–12 CLASSROOMS, Learning Sciences International, USA

Willingham, D. (2010), WHY DON'T STUDENTS LIKE SCHOOL?, Jossey-Bass, San Francisco, US

Willis, J. & Todorov, A. (2006), FIRST IMPRESSIONS: MAKING UP YOUR MIND AFTER A 100-MS EXPOSURE TO A FACE, Psychological Science, 17, 592-598.

APPENDIX A: THE EARLY CAREER FRAMEWORK

The Early Career Framework (ECF) sets out what early career teachers are entitled to learn about and learn how to do when they start their careers. It underpins a new entitlement for 2 years of professional development designed to help early career teachers develop their practice, knowledge and working habits.

A

1 High Expectations

Learn that...

1. Teachers have the ability to affect and improve the wellbeing, motivation and behaviour of their pupils.

2. Teachers are key role models, who can influence the attitudes, values and behaviours of their pupils.

3. Teacher expectations can affect pupil outcomes; setting goals that challenge and stretch pupils is essential.

4. Setting clear expectations can help communicate shared values that improve classroom and school culture.

5. A culture of mutual trust and respect supports effective relationships.

6. High-quality teaching has a long-term positive effect on pupils' life chances, particularly for children from disadvantaged backgrounds.

Learn how to...

Communicate a belief in the academic potential of all pupils, by:
Using intentional and consistent language that promotes challenge and aspiration.

Setting tasks that stretch pupils, but which are achievable, within a challenging curriculum.

Creating a positive environment where making mistakes and learning from them and the need for effort and perseverance are part of the daily routine.

Seeking opportunities to engage parents and carers in the education of their children (e.g. proactively highlighting successes).

Demonstrate consistently high behavioural expectations, by:
Creating a culture of respect and trust in the classroom that supports all pupils to succeed (e.g. by modelling the types of courteous behaviour expected of pupils).

Teaching and rigorously maintaining clear behavioural expectations (e.g. for contributions, volume level and concentration).

Applying rules, sanctions and rewards in line with school policy, escalating behaviour incidents as appropriate.

Acknowledging and praising pupil effort and emphasising progress being made.

2 | How Pupils Learn

Learn that...

1. Learning involves a lasting change in pupils' capabilities or understanding.

2. Prior knowledge plays an important role in how pupils learn; committing some key facts to their long-term memory is likely to help pupils learn more complex ideas.

3. An important factor in learning is memory, which can be thought of as comprising two elements: working memory and long-term memory.

4. Working memory is where information that is being actively processed is held, but its capacity is limited and can be overloaded.

5. Long-term memory can be considered as a store of knowledge that changes as pupils learn by integrating new ideas with existing knowledge.

6. Where prior knowledge is weak, pupils are more likely to develop misconceptions, particularly if new ideas are introduced too quickly.

7. Regular purposeful practice of what has previously been taught can help consolidate material and help pupils remember what they have learned.

8. Requiring pupils to retrieve information from memory, and spacing practice so that pupils revisit ideas after a gap are also likely to strengthen recall.

9. Worked examples that take pupils through each step of a new process are also likely to support pupils to learn.

Learn how to...

Avoid overloading working memory, by:

Taking into account pupils' prior knowledge when planning how much new information to introduce.

Breaking complex material into smaller steps (e.g. using partially completed examples to focus pupils on the specific steps).

Reducing distractions that take attention away from what is being taught (e.g. keeping the complexity of a task to a minimum, so that attention is focused on the content).

Build on pupils' prior knowledge, by:

Identifying possible misconceptions and planning how to prevent these forming.

Linking what pupils already know to what is being taught (e.g. explaining how new content builds on what is already known).

Sequencing lessons so that pupils secure foundational knowledge before encountering more complex content.

Encouraging pupils to share emerging understanding and points of confusion so that misconceptions can be addressed.

Increase likelihood of material being retained, by:

Balancing exposition, repetition, practice and retrieval of critical knowledge and skills.

Planning regular review and practice of key ideas and concepts over time.

Designing practice, generation and retrieval tasks that provide just enough support so that pupils experience a high success rate when attempting challenging work.

Increasing challenge with practice and retrieval as knowledge becomes more secure (e.g. by removing scaffolding, lengthening spacing or introducing interacting elements).

3 Subject and Curriculum

Learn that...

1. A school's curriculum enables it to set out its vision for the knowledge, skills and values that its pupils will learn, encompassing the national curriculum within a coherent wider vision for successful learning.

2. Secure subject knowledge helps teachers to motivate pupils and teach effectively.

3. Ensuring pupils master foundational concepts and knowledge before moving on is likely to build pupils' confidence and help them succeed.

4. Anticipating common misconceptions within particular subjects is also an important aspect of curricular knowledge; working closely with colleagues to develop an understanding of likely misconceptions is valuable.

5. Explicitly teaching pupils the knowledge and skills they need to succeed within particular subject areas is beneficial.

6. In order for pupils to think critically, they must have a secure understanding of knowledge within the subject area they are being asked to think critically about.

7. In all subject areas, pupils learn new ideas by linking those ideas to existing knowledge, organising this knowledge into increasingly complex mental models (or "schemata"); carefully sequencing teaching to facilitate this process is important.

8. Pupils are likely to struggle to transfer what has been learnt in one discipline to a new or unfamiliar context.

9. To access the curriculum, early literacy provides fundamental knowledge; reading comprises two elements: word reading and language comprehension; systematic synthetic phonics is the most effective approach for teaching pupils to decode.

10. Every teacher can improve pupils' literacy, including by explicitly teaching reading, writing and oral language skills specific to individual disciplines.

Learn how to...

Deliver a carefully sequenced and coherent curriculum, by:

Identifying essential concepts, knowledge, skills and principles of the subject and providing opportunity for all pupils to learn and master these critical components.

Ensuring pupils' thinking is focused on key ideas within the subject.

Working with experienced colleagues to accumulate and refine a collection of powerful analogies, illustrations, examples, explanations and demonstrations.

Using resources and materials aligned with the school curriculum (e.g. textbooks or shared resources designed by experienced colleagues that carefully sequence content).

Being aware of common misconceptions and discussing with experienced colleagues how to help pupils master important concepts.

Support pupils to build increasingly complex mental models, by:
Discussing curriculum design with experienced colleagues and balancing exposition, repetition, practice of critical skills and knowledge.

Revisiting the big ideas of the subject over time and teaching key concepts through a range of examples.

Drawing explicit links between new content and the core concepts and principles in the subject

Develop fluency, by:
Providing tasks that support pupils to learn key ideas securely (e.g. quizzing pupils so they develop fluency with times tables).

Using retrieval and spaced practice to build automatic recall of key knowledge.

Help pupils apply knowledge and skills to other contexts, by:
Ensuring pupils have relevant domain-specific knowledge, especially when being asked to think critically within a subject.

Interleaving concrete and abstract examples, slowly withdrawing concrete examples and drawing attention to the underlying structure of problems.

Develop pupils' literacy, by:
Demonstrating a clear understanding of systematic synthetic phonics, particularly if teaching early reading and spelling.

Supporting younger pupils to become fluent readers and to write fluently and legibly.

Teaching unfamiliar vocabulary explicitly and planning for pupils to be repeatedly exposed to high-utility and high-frequency vocabulary in what is taught.

Modelling reading comprehension by asking questions, making predictions, and summarising when reading.

Promoting reading for pleasure (e.g. by using a range of whole class reading approaches and regularly reading high-quality texts to children).

Modelling and requiring high-quality oral language, recognising that spoken language underpins the development of reading and writing (e.g. requiring pupils to respond to questions in full sentences, making use of relevant technical vocabulary).

Teaching different forms of writing by modelling planning, drafting and editing.

APPENDIX A: EARLY CAREER FRAMEWORK

4 Classroom Practice

Learn that...

1. Effective teaching can transform pupils' knowledge, capabilities and beliefs about learning.

2. Effective teachers introduce new material in steps, explicitly linking new ideas to what has been previously studied and learned.

3. Modelling helps pupils understand new processes and ideas; good models make abstract ideas concrete and accessible.

4. Guides, scaffolds and worked examples can help pupils apply new ideas, but should be gradually removed as pupil expertise increases.

5. Explicitly teaching pupils metacognitive strategies linked to subject knowledge, including how to plan, monitor and evaluate, supports independence and academic success.

6. Questioning is an essential tool for teachers; questions can be used for many purposes, including to check pupils' prior knowledge, assess understanding and break down problems.

7. High-quality classroom talk can support pupils to articulate key ideas, consolidate understanding and extend their vocabulary.

8. Practice is an integral part of effective teaching; ensuring pupils have repeated opportunities to practise, with appropriate guidance and support, increases success.

9. Paired and group activities can increase pupil success, but to work together effectively pupils need guidance, support and practice.

10. How pupils are grouped is also important; care should be taken to monitor the impact of groupings on pupil attainment, behaviour and motivation.

11. Homework can improve pupil outcomes, particularly for older pupils, but it is likely that the quality of homework and its relevance to main class teaching is more important than the amount set.

Learn how to...

Plan effective lessons, by:

Using modelling, explanations and scaffolds, acknowledging that novices need more structure early in a domain.

Enabling critical thinking and problem solving by first teaching the necessary foundational content knowledge.

Removing scaffolding only when pupils are achieving a high degree of success in applying previously taught material.

Providing sufficient opportunity for pupils to consolidate and practise applying new knowledge and skills.

Breaking tasks down into constituent components when first setting up independent practice (e.g. using tasks that scaffold pupils through meta-cognitive and procedural processes).

Make good use of expositions, by:
Starting expositions at the point of current pupil understanding.

Combining a verbal explanation with a relevant graphical representation of the same concept or process, where appropriate.

Using concrete representation of abstract ideas (e.g. making use of analogies, metaphors, examples and non-examples).

Model effectively, by:
Narrating thought processes when modelling to make explicit how experts think (e.g. asking questions aloud that pupils should consider when working independently and drawing pupils' attention to links with prior knowledge).

Making the steps in a process memorable and ensuring pupils can recall them (e.g. naming them, developing mnemonics, or linking to memorable stories).

Exposing potential pitfalls and explaining how to avoid them.

Stimulate pupil thinking and check for understanding, by:
Planning activities around what you want pupils to think hard about.

Including a range of types of questions in class discussions to extend and challenge pupils (e.g. by modelling new vocabulary or asking pupils to justify answers).

Providing appropriate wait time between question and response where more developed responses are required.

Considering the factors that will support effective collaborative or paired work (e.g. familiarity with routines, whether pupils have the necessary prior knowledge and how pupils are grouped).

Providing scaffolds for pupil talk to increase the focus and rigour of dialogue.

5 Adaptive Teaching

Learn that...

1. Pupils are likely to learn at different rates and to require different levels and types of support from teachers to succeed.

2. Seeking to understand pupils' differences, including their different levels of prior knowledge and potential barriers to learning, is an essential part of teaching.

3. Adapting teaching in a responsive way, including by providing targeted support to pupils who are struggling, is likely to increase pupil success.

4. Adaptive teaching is less likely to be valuable if it causes the teacher to artificially create distinct tasks for different groups of pupils or to set lower expectations for particular pupils.

5. Flexibly grouping pupils within a class to provide more tailored support can be effective, but care should be taken to monitor its impact on engagement and motivation, particularly for low attaining pupils.

6. There is a common misconception that pupils have distinct and identifiable learning styles. This is not supported by evidence and attempting to tailor lessons to learning styles is unlikely to be beneficial.

7. Pupils with special educational needs or disabilities are likely to require additional or adapted support; working closely with colleagues, families and pupils to understand barriers and identify effective strategies is essential.

Learn how to...

Develop an understanding of different pupil needs, by:

Identifying pupils who need new content further broken down.

Making use of formative assessment.

Working closely with the Special Educational Needs Co-ordinator (SENCO) and special education professionals and the Designated Safeguarding Lead.

Using the SEND Code of Practice, which provides additional guidance on supporting pupils with SEND effectively.

Provide opportunity for all pupils to experience success, by:

Adapting lessons, whilst maintaining high expectations for all, so that all pupils have the opportunity to meet expectations.

Balancing input of new content so that pupils master important concepts.

Making effective use of teaching assistants.

Meet individual needs without creating unnecessary workload, by:
Making use of well-designed resources (e.g. textbooks).

Planning to connect new content with pupils' existing knowledge or providing additional pre-teaching if pupils lack critical knowledge.

Building in additional practice or removing unnecessary expositions.

Reframing questions to provide greater scaffolding or greater stretch.

Considering carefully whether intervening within lessons with individuals and small groups would be more efficient and effective than planning different lessons for different groups of pupils.

Group pupils effectively, by:
Applying high expectations to all groups, and ensuring all pupils have access to a rich curriculum.

Changing groups regularly, avoiding the perception that groups are fixed.

Ensuring that any groups based on attainment are subject specific.

APPENDIX A: EARLY CAREER FRAMEWORK

6 Assessment

Learn that...

1. Effective assessment is critical to teaching because it provides teachers with information about pupils' understanding and needs.

2. Good assessment helps teachers avoid being over-influenced by potentially misleading factors, such as how busy pupils appear.

3. Before using any assessment, teachers should be clear about the decision it will be used to support and be able to justify its use.

4. To be of value, teachers use information from assessments to inform the decisions they make; in turn, pupils must be able to act on feedback for it to have an effect.

5. High-quality feedback can be written or verbal; it is likely to be accurate and clear, encourage further effort, and provide specific guidance on how to improve.

6. Over time, feedback should support pupils to monitor and regulate their own learning.

7. Working with colleagues to identify efficient approaches to assessment is important; assessment can become onerous and have a disproportionate impact on workload.

Learn how to...

Avoid common assessment pitfalls, by:

Planning formative assessment tasks linked to lesson objectives and thinking ahead about what would indicate understanding (e.g. by using hinge questions to pinpoint knowledge gaps).

Drawing conclusions about what pupils have learned by looking at patterns of performance over a number of assessments (e.g. appreciating that assessments draw inferences about learning from performance).

Choosing, where possible, externally validated materials, used in controlled conditions when required to make summative assessments.

Check prior knowledge and understanding during lessons, by:

Using assessments to check for prior knowledge and pre-existing misconceptions.

Structuring tasks and questions to enable the identification of knowledge gaps and misconceptions (e.g. by using common misconceptions within multiple-choice questions).

Prompting pupils to elaborate when responding to questioning to check that a correct answer stems from secure understanding.

Monitoring pupil work during lessons, including checking for misconceptions.

Provide high-quality feedback, by:
Focusing on specific actions for pupils and providing time for pupils to respond to feedback.

Appreciating that pupils' responses to feedback can vary depending on a range of social factors (e.g. the message the feedback contains or the age of the child).

Scaffolding self-assessment by sharing model work with pupils, highlighting key details.

Thinking carefully about how to ensure feedback is specific and helpful when using peer- or self-assessment.

Make marking manageable and effective, by:
Recording data only when it is useful for improving pupil outcomes.

Working with colleagues to identify efficient approaches to marking and alternative approaches to providing feedback (e.g. using whole class feedback or well supported peer- and self-assessment).

Using verbal feedback during lessons in place of written feedback after lessons where possible.

Understanding that written marking is only one form of feedback.

Reducing the opportunity cost of marking (e.g. by using abbreviations and codes in written feedback).

Prioritising the highlighting of errors related to misunderstandings, rather than careless mistakes when marking.

7 Managing Behaviour

Learn that...

1. Establishing and reinforcing routines, including through positive reinforcement, can help create an effective learning environment.

2. A predictable and secure environment benefits all pupils, but is particularly valuable for pupils with special educational needs.

3. The ability to self-regulate one's emotions affects pupils' ability to learn, success in school and future lives.

4. Teachers can influence pupils' resilience and beliefs about their ability to succeed, by ensuring all pupils have the opportunity to experience meaningful success.

5. Building effective relationships is easier when pupils believe that their feelings will be considered and understood.

6. Pupils are motivated by intrinsic factors (related to their identity and values) and extrinsic factors (related to reward).

7. Pupils' investment in learning is also driven by their prior experiences and perceptions of success and failure.

Learn how to...

Develop a positive, predictable and safe environment for pupils, by:

Establishing a supportive and inclusive environment with a predictable system of reward and sanction in the classroom.

Working alongside colleagues as part of a wider system of behaviour management (e.g. recognising responsibilities and understanding the right to assistance and training from senior colleagues).

Giving manageable, specific and sequential instructions.

Checking pupils' understanding of instructions before a task begins.

Using consistent language and non-verbal signals for common classroom directions.

Using early and least-intrusive interventions as an initial response to low level disruption.

Responding quickly to any behaviour or bullying that threatens emotional safety.

Establish effective routines and expectations, by:
Creating and explicitly teaching routines in line with the school ethos that maximise time for learning (e.g. setting and reinforcing expectations about key transition points).

Practising routines at the beginning of the school year.

Reinforcing routines (e.g. by articulating the link between time on task and success).

Build trusting relationships, by:
Liaising with parents, carers and colleagues to better understand pupils' individual circumstances and how they can be supported to meet high academic and behavioural expectations.

Responding consistently to pupil behaviour.

Motivate pupils, by:
Supporting pupils to master challenging content, which builds towards long-term goals.

Providing opportunities for pupils to articulate their long-term goals and helping them to see how these are related to their success in school.

Helping pupils to journey from needing extrinsic motivation to being motivated to work intrinsically.

8	Professional Behaviours

Learn that...

1. Effective professional development is likely to be sustained over time, involve expert support or coaching and opportunities for collaboration.

2. Reflective practice, supported by feedback from and observation of experienced colleagues, professional debate, and learning from educational research, is also likely to support improvement.

3. Teachers can make valuable contributions to the wider life of the school in a broad range of ways, including by supporting and developing effective professional relationships with colleagues.

4. Building effective relationships with parents, carers and families can improve pupils' motivation, behaviour and academic success.

5. Teaching assistants (TAs) can support pupils more effectively when they are prepared for lessons by teachers, and when TAs supplement rather than replace support from teachers.

6. SENCOs, pastoral leaders, careers advisors and other specialist colleagues also have valuable expertise and can ensure that appropriate support is in place for pupils.

7. Engaging in high-quality professional development can help teachers improve.

Learn how to...

Develop as a professional, by:

Engaging in professional development focused on developing an area of practice with clear intentions for impact on pupil outcomes, sustained over time with built-in opportunities for practice.

Strengthening pedagogical and subject knowledge by participating in wider networks.

Seeking challenge, feedback and critique from mentors and other colleagues in an open and trusting working environment.

Engaging critically with research and discussing evidence with colleagues.

Reflecting on progress made, recognising strengths and weaknesses and identifying next steps for further improvement.

Build effective working relationships, by:

Contributing positively to the wider school culture and developing a feeling of shared responsibility for improving the lives of all pupils within the school.

Seeking ways to support individual colleagues and working as part of a team.

Communicating with parents and carers proactively and making effective use of parents' evenings to engage parents and carers in their children's schooling.

Working closely with the SENCO and other professionals supporting pupils with additional needs, making explicit links between interventions delivered outside of lessons with classroom teaching.

Sharing the intended lesson outcomes with teaching assistants ahead of lessons.

Ensuring that support provided by teaching assistants in lessons is additional to, rather than a replacement for, support from the teacher.

Knowing who to contact with any safeguarding concerns.

Manage workload and wellbeing, by:
Using and personalising systems and routines to support efficient time and task management.

Understanding the right to support (e.g. to deal with misbehaviour).

Collaborating with colleagues to share the load of planning and preparation and making use of shared resources (e.g. textbooks).

Protecting time for rest and recovery.

APPENDIX B: TEACHERS' STANDARDS

These are the Teachers' Standards for use in schools in England from September 2012. The standards define the minimum level of practice expected of trainees and teachers from the point of being awarded qualified teacher status (QTS).

The Teachers' Standards are used to assess all trainees working towards QTS, and all those completing their statutory induction period. They are also used to assess the performance of all teachers with QTS who are subject to The Education (School Teachers' Appraisal) (England) Regulations 2012, and may additionally be used to assess the performance of teachers who are subject to these regulations and who hold qualified teacher learning and skills (QTLS) status.